A pocket guide to

PALMS

A pocket guide to

PALMS

Martin Gibbons

CHARTWELL
BOOKS, INC.

DEDICATION

I dedicate this book to my wonderful wife, Emma

ACKNOWLEDGMENTS

The publisher is indebted to the following people and organizations for kindly supplying all the photography for this book:

Martin Gibbons, Tobias W. Spanner, Brian Trollip, Montgomery Botanical Center, Old Cutler Road, Miami Florida, USA, Inge Hoffmann, Huntington Botanical Gardens, San Marino, California, USA, Catherine Clarkin, David Jones, Royal Botanic Gardens, Kew, Richmond, Surrey, UK, Sadek Tazi, Brian Laughland, Fairchild Tropical Garden, Coral Gables (Miami), Florida, USA, Mark Katz, Lakeside Palmetum, Oakland, California, USA, Pauleen Sullivan, Bill Dickenson, Ian Hutton, Dick Endt, Nic Broyer, Nick Turland, Jim Wright, Nguyen Van Du and Phuong Anh, Wilko Karmelk and Ganesh Mani Pradhan.

The front cover photograph (main picture) was supplied courtesy of © Gary Braasch/CORBIS.

This edition published in 2003 by
CHARTWELL BOOKS, INC.
A division of BOOK SALES, INC
114 Northfield Avenue,
Edison, New Jersey 08837

Produced by
PRC Publishing Ltd,
64 Brewery Road, London N7 9NT

A member of **Chrysalis** Books plc

ISBN 0 7858 1562 7

Printed and bound in Malaysia

Contents

Preface

I am in the happy and fortunate position of being able to earn a living from something that I enjoy so much. My interest in palms began some twenty years ago when I watered to death the first palm I ever owned. Learning to look after its replacement woke something in me that was to lead to a hobby, a passion, a successful business, and a life much of which has been spent traveling to and around some of the world's most exciting and beautiful countries in a never ending search for palms. That search has taken me to China, India, much of South America and Southeast Asia, South Africa, Mexico, Morocco, in fact most places where palms grow. Much of this traveling has been in the company of Tobias Spanner of Germany. On different expeditions we have been arrested in China and in the Sudan (where we were suspected of being CIA spies), stuck overnight in axle-deep mud trying to cross the Andes (twice) and broken down crossing the Nubian Desert, all good fun, though it didn't seem so at the time. During our travels we have been lucky enough to discover four species of *Trachycarpus* new to science, the latest in North Vietnam.

This pocket book is designed to whet the appetite of prospective palm enthusiasts and to appeal to those already bitten by the palm bug. At best, it can only scratch the surface of the subject, and covers a highly personal list of 200 species. Most of these I have seen in the wild and most of the photos have been taken in habitat. Others have been taken in botanic gardens, principally Fairchild Tropical Garden and the Montgomery Botanical Center, both in Florida, to whom I am grateful.

I would also like to thank those who lent pictures or allowed their palms to be photographed, Toby Spanner for helping to edit the text, Werner Schwab for checking the cycad section and all the many great friends I have made while pursuing this most wonderful of hobbies.

Martin Gibbons, The Palm Centre, Richmond, UK.

Right: This naturally branching Hyphaene *was photographed in Africa.*

Introduction

Palms, for most people, are the very essence of the tropics. Everyone knows coconut palms, having seen them fringing white sandy beaches on exotic holidays, and the date palm is equally well known. In fact, the palm tree has come to symbolize everything tropical, and its familiar form is used to advertise everything from cars to chocolate bars, vacations to vehicle hire, and liquor to lap tops. Beyond the date and the coconut though, most people's knowledge is fairly limited; they would be surprised to learn that there are almost 3,000 species of palm and more are being discovered all the time. And far from all occurring in equatorial rainforest, swampy jungle, or arid desert, there are hundreds which grow a long way from the equator in conditions considerably less than tropical.

Palms are monocotyledonous plants and most have a single woody trunk and complex leaves that emerge entire. Just a few branch naturally (see previous page) though some branch as a result of physical damage (right). Neither the trunk nor the leaves have the ability to expand once formed and it is this, among other things, that separates palms from other trees. The distinctive crown stays more or less the same size during the palm's life and is simply raised by the increasing height of the trunk.

Plants recognizable as palms first appeared on earth some 65 million years ago and associations between related species now geographically distant

Above: This Trachycarpus *in Kunming, China, has four or five "branches."*

from one another can be explained by continental drift. Pollen from many tropical palms has been found in Britain in the London clay, and countless other fossil records from all over the world indicate a climate very different from today's.

Andean wax palms (*Ceroxylon*) are among the tallest trees on the planet, at up to 200 feet (60m) (right). The double coconut (*Lodoicea*) produces the heaviest seed, which may be up to 44 lb (20kg) in weight, while the seeds of *Washingtonia* are scarcely bigger than a match head. Some palms, such as *Jubaea* and *Borassus*, have massive trunks (see page 10), while some *Syagrus* and *Chamaedorea* species are tiny, even at maturity (see page 11).

Economically palms are an extremely important group. Coconuts (see pages 12–13) and dates have already been mentioned. Add to these wax, timber for building, rattan for furniture, palm oil, leaves for thatching, pharmaceutical drugs, sago, sugar, alcohoholic "toddy," palm "honey," among other things, and it will be seen how important palms are, particularly in developing countries where they are either used locally (see page 14) or their products exported in exchange for other goods or foreign currency. Malaysia alone annually exports millions of dollars worth of palm oil (from *Elaeis guinieensis*) for use in cooking, soaps and lubricants, and thousands of tonnes of Carnauba wax from the *Copernicia* palm are exported every year

Above: Some Ceroxylon *palms can grow to 200 feet (60m). This one is about 130 feet (40m).*

A Pocket Guide to Palms

from Brazil for polishes and waxes. Rattan is a huge industry too. So called "cane" furniture is usually not made from bamboo as is frequently supposed, but from the flexible stems of climbing palms (rattans), mainly species of *Calamus* which grow in many tropical countries such as Malaysia, Indonesia, and the Philippines. In the past the raw material was usually exported unfinished, these days local industry usually

Above: This tiny Syagrus *species, already fruiting, is one of the smallest palms.*
Left: The author provides a sense of scale for Jubaea chilensis *in Chile, perhaps the largest palm trunks in the world.*

A Pocket Guide to Palms

Left: A coconut plantation in Burma.

Above: In China, the leaves of Trachycarpus nanus *are bundled together to make a broom.*

manufactures the finished item, retaining the added value for the exporting country.

Horticulture is playing an increasingly important role in the exploitation of palms and hundreds of thousands are sold annually for home use. In Europe, the Netherlands leads this market and many if not most of the palms seen for sale in supermarkets come from there (right). Within living memory, the number of palms available from garden nurseries has leapt from a mere handful to a wide range, and many are now routinely sold at florists' shops, service station forecourts, and chain stores.

While it is true that most palms occur in the tropics, they are found in every continent except Antarctica and some grow almost as close to the poles as they do to the equator. *Chamaerops humilis* in Europe is the record holder in this respect, at 44 degrees north, while its counterpart in the southern hemisphere is *Rhopalostylis sapida* on Chatham Island, New Zealand, at almost the same latitude. Unsurprisingly, because of their distance from the equator, these are rather hardy individuals, but others are cool tolerant for different reasons. Many palms occur in deserts and while these may be blazing hot during the day they are often bitterly cold at night. This resistance to cold may make them suitable for growing in temperate climates. *Brahea* and *Nannorrhops* are good examples. Others occur at high altitudes. The Andes Mountains of South America are home to a number of species which show promise as cultivated plants, and the beautiful blue *Chamaerops humilis* var. *cerifera* from the High Atlas in Morocco grows near the snow line and is impervious to even bitter cold. Perhaps the most popular cold hardy palm is *Trachycarpus fortunei* (page 16) from China which can tolerate 5 °F (–15 °C).

A Pocket Guide to Palms

Above: Kentia seedlings are potted up by the hundreds of thousands in a Dutch nursery for the European market.

Many other palms can be induced to grow in less than ideal conditions. There is much interest worldwide in the hobby of "growing palms where they shouldn't grow" and this has increased enormously over the last twenty years. Many societies of like-minded enthusiasts have sprung up, but there is still a seemingly unquenchable thirst for knowledge on the subject. As recently as the 1960s, the number of palm books available could be counted on the fingers of one hand, now there are hundreds. The internet has also played a huge part in disseminating information and these days seeds, books, and indeed, palms themselves can readily be bought on-line, feeding the growing demand. It is an exciting trend and with what look like major changes in the world's weather patterns, not least global warming, who knows where this interest in palms might lead.

Below: Trachycarpus fortunei *in the snow, the author's garden, central London, UK.*

The Cultivation of Palms

Broadly speaking palms can be propagated in one of two ways. Suckering or clustering species can be divided and as long as there are some roots on each portion, they usually carry on growing without setback. *Chamaerops humilis* clumps can be butchered with a chainsaw and still seem not to mind too much. They should be given a thorough watering a day or two before the operation commences and should be kept moist, humid, and out of direct sunlight thereafter, until new growth is detected.

Most palms, and certainly all solitary species, are propagated from seed. This can take anything from a few days (*Washingtonia*) to months or even years (*Acrocomia*). The principles are the same for all species. Seeds must be ripe for germination to succeed. Cut a sample seed in half with a pair of secateurs and examine the cut surface. If it is hard, not able to be dented with a thumbnail for example, then it is ripe enough to sow.

Where possible, seeds should be collected from the tree itself rather than from the ground. Obviously this is not always possible, but float testing the seeds should determine which have the best chance of germinating. In most cases, those that float should be discarded. Fresh seeds have a better success rate than those that have been stored, but many have a long viability. Desert species especially, such as *Brahea*, *Washingtonia*, and *Phoenix*, may still sprout after many months or even years, while the viability of rainforest palms, such as *Calamus* and *Pigafetta*, can be measured in days. Outer flesh sometimes contains chemical inhibitors which prevent the seed from germinating too soon. This should be removed, which may be very easy (*Jubaea*) or extremely difficult (*Areca catechu*, *Parajubaea*). In most cases, the seeds should be soaked for a few days, or at least overnight, before sowing. Some seeds should not be sown fresh (*Butia, Parajubaea*) and benefit from storage for a few weeks or months, some say until the seed rattles.

The most popular way of germinating palm seeds is known as the bag method. Mix the cleaned, soaked seeds with a moist medium and place in a clear, strong

Above: These cleaned Sabal uresana *seeds are ready to sow.*

plastic bag which should then be sealed and labeled. Coconut compost is ideal for this purpose for two reasons: it is uniformly dark so roots emerging from the seed can be easily seen, and secondly, it is light and airy, allowing oxygen as well as moisture to reach the seeds. If one or two drops only of water can be squeezed from a fistful of compost, then this is the right moisture content. If none can be, then add a little more water and try again. If too much water can be squeezed out, then add some dry compost to correct the imbalance. The bag should then be kept at a temperature consistent with the climate of the palm's habitat. Tropical species require up to 90 °F

(30 ℃), while those from temperate climates, such as *Ceroxylon* and *Trachycarpus*, need no heat at all, and indeed, may not germinate in other than cool conditions.

Germination can take a few days or many months to occur. Examine the bag regularly, perhaps once a week, and look out for the white root which will emerge from the seed. Some growers prefer to leave the young plant until the first leaves have formed. The

Above: The new roots can be seen through the plastic bag.

Below: This seedling of Chamaedorea microspadix *is ready to be potted up.*

sprouts should be removed and potted up into individual pots, again using the plant's origin as a guide as to which substrate to use. Many growers have their own preferred mixture, but as a general rule sandy, loamy soil is best for desert and savanna species, while those from the rainforest prefer something a little more peaty. That said, it is not uncommon to see totally the reverse in cultivated palms, so it may not be critical. In short, the soil should be able to hold moisture without staying waterlogged and

Above: For potting up seedlings, the soil mix should hold moisture but be airy.

*Right: Potted up, this seedling
is ready to face the world.*

yet be sufficiently airy to allow oxygen to permeate. Once potted up the young plant should be moved to a position in brighter, though indirect light. It will not require feeding at this stage as there will be sufficient nutrients within the seed to last it for some time. As it grows, it should be potted on into a larger pot.

Interior plants should be found a bright, permanent indoor position, out of draughts and direct sunlight. Little maintenance is required other than regular watering, an occasional feed and, once in a while, the removal of any dead lower leaves. Keep the leaves clean by putting the plant in the shower every so often to wash the dust away. Do not use leaf shine spray. Keep a close watch out for pests. The most common ones are red spider mite, mealy bug, and scale insects, which need to be treated appropriately.

For those intended for planting direct in the ground, as a general rule, wait until the roots fill a 6 inch (15cm) pot before doing so; plants smaller than this get off to a very slow start. In most cases, young plants will appreciate shade for the first few months or years. After that, again, use the plant's origins as a guide. Take care with positioning a young palm. What starts off as a seedling can, with some species, and especially in the tropics, rapidly turn into a monster.

Many palms transplant easily. You only have to look at the way some species are transplanted, especially in the USA, with tiny rootballs, to understand how tolerant they are of disturbance. To move a palm in the domestic setting, it should be watered for a few days before the move to enable maximum water take up. If there is sufficient time available, and ideally during spring or summer, it should then be "trenched" or "part-trenched." This involves digging with a spade, in a circle around the trunk and at an appropriate distance from it, cutting through any roots that are encountered. This job may be completed in two halves with a gap of a few weeks in between. The trench so formed should then be back filled with soil and the tree kept well-watered

Right: A healthy crop of Chamaedorea microspadix
seedlings.

Above: Large palms should be handled with care. In some cases a small crane or similar may be necessary to move them safely.

A Pocket Guide to Palms

for a period of time, ideally three months. During this time the palm will replace the cut roots with new ones, within the soil ball that has been created. When this time has elapsed, the trench should be re-opened, the root ball undercut and the palm lifted for transfer to its new location. Warning: palms can be extremely heavy and the weight of even a medium-sized specimen should not be underestimated. A small crane may turn out to be necessary to enable the job to be done efficiently and, above all, safely (see left).

Palms in the ground require a little more maintenance than those in the home. In the tropics especially, they can grow really quickly and this will be accompanied by a great deal of debris as old leaves fall. Leaves can be lopped or trimmed before they fall, as can unwanted inflorescences. Exterior palms can be fertilized heavily, especially during the growing season, and of course, well watered if the weather is dry.

Palms

Acoelorrhaphe wrightii
Everglades palm

Features
An easily recognized clumping palm, frequently cultivated in Florida where it is used to grace parks and gardens. The only species in the genus, it grows to about 13 feet (4m) high, usually with a few taller trunks dominating the rest. The leaves are fan shaped, bright green above and silvery below; the slim trunks are covered with old leaf bases, and the leaf stalks are spiny. The small round fruits are up to ½ inch (1cm) in diameter and red/brown, turning black when fully ripe. It occurs naturally in the western Caribbean region, just creeping into southern Florida, and is often found growing near fresh water or in swamps.

Cultivation
Easy to cultivate, the fresh seeds germinate without difficulty and seedling growth is moderately fast. If a yellowing of the leaves occurs, this can be corrected with an acid fertilizer. Requires sub-tropical to tropical conditions, though may tolerate the occasional light frost.

Right: Acoelorrhaphe wrightii, *cultivated, National Tropical Botanical Garden, Kalaheo, Kauai, Hawaii.*

Acrocomia aculeata
Coyol palm

Features

One of only two species in the genus, it is an extremely spiny, solitary palm, growing to 35 feet (10m) or so, with an often slightly swollen trunk covered with sharp spines. It has long, feather-shaped leaves, slightly plumose in appearance, yellow flowers, and round fruits up to 2 inches (5cm) in diameter that are greenish-yellow, the skin splitting when fully ripe. It is common throughout its range from Brazil through to Mexico and Cuba, where it grows in savanna and open woodland, usually at low altitudes.

Cultivation

The seeds are difficult to germinate and different methods have been suggested for hastening the process. These include filing or cracking the hard seed coat, soaking in water for long periods, and treating with acid. Frustratingly they seem to germinate easily enough in the wild and seedlings are often seen growing under the parent tree. Once germinated, seedling growth is quite fast and the first spines soon appear.

Above: Acrocomia aculeata *seen in its natural habitat, Nayarit, Mexico.*
Left: Close-up of the spine covered trunk.

Adonidia merrillii (syn. Veitchia)
Christmas palm

Features

From the Philippine islands, this tropical palm (one of about twenty species in the genus) derives its name from the bright, carmine-red fruits that appear at Christmas time. They are naturally solitary palms (though often planted in twos or threes in cultivation), growing to about 20 or 25 feet (6 or 7m) in height. The tapering trunks have clearly visible old leaf scars and the prominent crown shaft is green. The feather-shaped leaves, which curl in on themselves along their length, are dull green above and whitish below. The red fruits are oval and 1 inch (3cm) long and are borne in large numbers below the crown shaft. These attractive small palms are widely planted as street trees in the tropics and are also used in shopping malls. They will not tolerate frost.

Cultivation

The fresh seeds germinate readily and subsequent seedling growth is also fast.

Left: Adonidia merrillii is commonly used as a street tree, Florida Keys.

Aiphanes aculeata
(syn. A. caryotifolia)
Coyure palm

Features

This is the best known member of a large genus of
small spiny palms native to the northwest of South
America. It has a slim, solitary trunk to some 30
feet (10m) and the dark green feather leaves have clustered, plumose leaflets with
blunt tips, which are somewhat wedge-shaped, giving a ruffled appearance. All
parts of the palm are covered in spines. The fruits, ½ or ¾ inch (1 or 2cm) in diameter and borne in pendulous bunches are bright red at maturity and often the first
thing to attract attention in the gloomy forest where it occurs.

Cultivation

Alas, not widely cultivated because of its spiny nature
but if sited carefully, this small palm is a valuable addition
to the tropical garden or, when young, the heated conservatory. The seeds are easy to germinate and seedling
growth is fast. According to the literature, it was popular
in England as a glasshouse plant in Victorian times.

Above: Aiphanes aculeata, *cultivated near Quevedo, Ecuador.*
Left: The orange-red fruits.

Aiphanes verrucosa

Features

A rare and attractive relative of *Aiphanes aculeata* that is known only from one tiny population in Ecuador, growing on the "Inca Trail," where it is under severe threat from deforestation and agriculture. The altitude is quite high there, at least 8,000 feet (2,500m), which suggests that this endangered palm may be slightly more cold-tolerant than its cousins. It has clustered stems to about 15 feet (5m) tall, with but a few feather leaves, the leaflets being flat in arrangement. As with others in the genus, all parts of the palm are covered with sharp spines. Mature fruits are about 1 inch (3cm) in diameter, greenish white, and corky in appearance, tending to split when ripe.

Cultivation

Practically unknown in cultivation, further attempts should be made to introduce this palm from the wild. As in so many other cases, it may well be the only way it will survive.

Above: Aiphanes verrucosa *in habitat on the "Inca Trail,"*
   Villacabamba, Ecuador
Right: The fruits are corky when ripe.

Allagoptera arenaria
Restinga palm

Features

One of a genus of four species, this interesting palm grows in large colonies on sand dunes near the coast in southeastern Brazil. It is low-growing and solitary stemmed, the trunks either subterranean or horizontal. The leaflets on the pinnate leaves are irregularly arranged in groups in different planes and are somewhat curly giving an unusual and plumose appearance. Additionally, the fruits are held on erect infructescences rather like corn-on-the-cob. With these characteristics, the genus is unmistakable. The fruits are ½ or ¾ inch (1 or 2cm) long, oval in shape, greenish-yellow, and rather difficult to tell when ripe.

Cultivation

The seeds are erratic to germinate, and seedling growth is slow to begin with but speeds up once the plant is established. Requires a sandy soil and good light. An attractive, small growing palm ideal for the tropical or subtropical coastal garden. May also be able to stand light frost.

Above: Allagoptera arenaria *in habitat, Espirito Santo, Brazil.*
Left: The corn-on-the-cob-like fruit.

Allagoptera campestris

Buri palm

Features

Similar in appearance to *A. arenaria*, though smaller, this pretty palm grows at much higher altitudes so may safely be considered a little more cold-tolerant. Found inland from the Brazil coast at up to an elevation of 5,000 feet (1,500m), it covers some areas as far as the eye can see, for perhaps hundreds of square miles. The trunks are short and may be underground, the leaflets are curly and plumose, usually split at the tip, and the greenish yellow fruits, which are held upright on corncob like structures, are oval in shape and ½ inch (1cm) or so in length.

Cultivation

As is so often the case, while so common in the wild these palms are inexplicably rare in cultivation, yet would be perfect for the smaller garden in warm climates and

elsewhere as an unusual conservatory palm. The seeds germinate over a period of some months and the seedlings are slow to establish themselves.

Above: Allagoptera campestris *seen in habitat, Minas Gerais, Brazil.*
Left: The distinctive fruits are held erect.

Archontophoenix alexandrae

King palm, Alexandra palm

Features

Popular Australian palm widely cultivated across the world for both indoor and out-door use. Solitary, it grows to around 70 feet (20m) tall, with a slim, ringed trunk often swollen at the base. The leaves are feather-shaped, bright green, with silvery whitish undersides, and they are carried perpendicular to the ground. The fruits are borne in large clusters below the mid-green crownshaft and they are bright red when ripe. It occurs naturally in Queensland where it grows in a range of habitats from lowland swamps to wet moun-tainous areas.

Cultivation

The small seeds of this fast growing palm are quick to germinate and sub-sequent growth is also fast, given its preferred conditions of rich and moist soil, and atmospheric humidity. It will tolerate only light frosts. It is often sold as a houseplant and may succeed given a humid location with bright light.

Right: Archontophoenix alexandrae,

cultivated, Thailand.

Archontophoenix cunninghamiana
Bangalow palm

Features

Broadly similar to *A. alexandrae,* it may be distinguished from it by the green (as opposed to silver) undersides to its pinnate leaves and the distinctive crownshaft, which is more often brown than green. It is a tall, solitary, slim-trunked palm growing to 70 feet (20m) or more and occurs in the rainforests of northeastern Australia. It too produces fruits in large numbers, which are bright red when ripe. Popular around the world, it is a handsome, fast-growing species and looks well in the garden in warmer climates. There are six species in the genus, but this number has increased recently as "forms" have been found to deserve species status.

Cultivation

This is probably the most cold-tolerant of the genus, though none can be considered hardy in the true sense of the word. The small seeds germinate quickly and easily and the subsequent growth of the seedling is also very fast.

Right: Archontophoenix cunninghamiana, *cultivated, Porto Allegre Botanical Gardens, Brazil.*

A Pocket Guide to Palms

Areca vestiaria

Orange crownshaft palm

Features

A highly ornamental tropical palm blessed with a bright orange crownshaft, and bearing fruits, ¾ or 1 inch (2 or 3cm) long, which are also orange. From Indonesia, where it lives in swampy forests, it is a clumping species that produces stilt roots and dark green, pinnate leaves with broad leaflets. It grows to about 30 feet (10m) and the trunk is slim and clearly ringed with the scars of old leaves. A red form has recently made its appearance in cultivation which has dark red new leaves and is a very attractive palm.

Cultivation

The seeds are hard to clean but easy to germinate, and the young plants grow quickly. Essentially tropical in their requirements, they can also tolerate low temperatures for short periods but are most suitable either for the tropical garden or the heated conservatory. They show some promise as houseplants, but attention should be paid to humidity; they will not thrive in dry air.

Above: Areca vestiaria, cultivated, Rio de Janiero Botanical Gardens, Brazil.
Left: The orange crownshafts.

Arenga engleri
Taiwan arenga

Features

A pretty and adaptable palm which shows
some promise of cold hardiness but also
succeeds well in the tropics. It is a clumping species with pinnate leaves, the leaflets
are long and narrow, with silvery undersides and uneven, notched tips. The maximum height is probably no more than 10
feet (3m) and individual trunks die after flowering and fruiting, to be replaced by others. The abundant fruits, either red, yellow, or orange, contain caustic crystals and
should be handled with care.

Cultivation

The seeds germinate readily and the young plants grow easily and quickly. They are
attractive at all stages and make nice house plants for a few years, though require
humidity to prosper. An excellent lawn specimen, which tolerates sun or shade, and

may well be tried in the sheltered, temperate garden where, though slow-
growing, it will tolerate a few degrees
of frost.

Above: Arenga engleri, *cultivated, Hong Kong
   Botanical Gardens.*
Left: The red and yellow fruits.

Arenga hookeriana
Hooker's arenga

Features

A lovely, small, tropical palm, native to Malaysia and Thailand, which bears extraordinary and instantly recognizable leaves in a whole variety of shapes and sizes, some long and narrow, some big and broad with wavy margins. The plants stay quite small, to perhaps 6 or 7 feet (2m) or so, with many slim cane-like stems. The small fruits are round, and red when ripe.

Cultivation

Succeeds well in the tropical garden and also as a pot or tub plant in the heated conservatory or glass house. Makes an interesting houseplant too, provided attention is paid to humidity and the plant is kept out of direct sunlight. In the garden it seems to do best if shaded or semi-shaded, reflecting its forest understory origins.

Above: Arenga hookeriana, cultivated, Malaysia.
Left: The wavy leaves are instantly recognizable.

Arenga pinnata
Sugar palm

Features

This is a big, up to 80 feet (25m), rather untidy, and solitary tropical palm, which has a thick, black trunk covered with old leaf bases and blunt spines that may be nearly 2 feet (0.5m) long. The leaves are pinnate and dark green. Fast growing, it is widely cultivated in Southeast Asia for the sugary sap, which is gathered from the cut inflorescences. In common with the other 20 or so species in the genus, the trunk dies after flowering and fruiting. Fruits—purplish black when ripe—are produced in huge numbers on long, pendulous infructescences, and contain stinging crystals.

Cultivation

Fast growing, this palm succeeds well in the tropics given rich soil and a good supply of water. Requires plenty of room, and an eye should be kept on it as the big trunks die after flowering.

Above: Arenga pinnata,
cultivated, Florida.
Far left: Close up of the
fibrous trunk.
Left: The inflorescence,
about to flower.

Astrocaryum alatum

Coquito palm

Features

Unusual South American palm with nominally pinnate leaves, but with the broad leaflets so close together that the leaves appear almost entire from a distance. This, together with its strangely arching, swept back look gives the palm an unmistakable appearance. It grows to about 15 or 20 feet (5 or 6m) tall and the trunk is solitary. All parts of the tree are covered with spines. From the east coasts of Costa Rica, Panama, and Nicaragua, it is not uncommonly seen in rainforest at low elevation. The flower stalks grow among the leaves, after flowering they produce round fruits about ¾ to 1 inch (2 to 3cm) in diameter, which are yellow-brown when ripe.

Cultivation

This unique palm is almost unknown in cultivation, which is a great shame as it would be a valuable addition to any tropical or sub-tropical garden, however care should be taken with siting in view of its spiny nature. The egg-shaped seeds, unlike others in the genus, are fast and easy to germinate.

Above: Juvenile plants in cultivation, Lundkvist Garden, Hawaii.

Left: Astrocaryum alatum, *in habitat, Costa Rica.*

Astrocaryum standleyanum

Features

A handsome if spiny palm from the northwestern corner of South America, growing to some 30 feet (10m) or more, with a solitary trunk and a crown of dark green, plumose, pinnate leaves that are also spiny. The trunk itself is stout and covered with short, flat, black spines, which protect against predatory animals. The orange-red fruits are produced in great numbers in large, pendulous clusters and are fed to farm animals locally. This palm is often left when forest is cleared for pasture, though whether it can reproduce under these conditions is not certain.

Cultivation

The hard seeds have star-shaped marks on one end, hence the scientific name. They are rather difficult to germinate and various methods have been suggested to speed up the process. Once sprouted, the young plants grow steadily and are soon covered with spines. This makes a wonderful ornamental palm if care is taken to plant it away from paths and public access.

Above: Astrocaryum standleyanum, *in habitat, Ecuador.*
Left: The fruits and spine detail.

Attalea colenda

Features

A very large, up to 100 feet (30m) tall, solitary, tropical palm from Colombia and Ecuador with a thick trunk and long, upright pinnate leaves, like a huge shuttlecock. Not uncommon within its lowland range, in some areas it is a prominent feature of the landscape and grows in dense colonies. The large oily fruits (oval, and up to 2 inches (6cm) long) hang down from among the leaves in huge carrot-shaped clusters and are pale brown when ripe.

Cultivation

The big seeds are slow and erratic to germinate but the seedlings grow quite fast. This massive palm is sadly underused in the warm climates where it would thrive. It would make the most stunning addition to the tropical garden or park where its large form could be best appreciated. They are, however, slowly beginning to appear in the collections of palm enthusiasts and hopefully this will spread to municipal use as their qualities are appreciated.

Above: Attalea colenda, in habitat, Ecuador.
Left: The large fruits hang down in huge carrot-shaped clusters.

Attalea funifera
Piassaba palm

Features

An unmistakable, large, upright, solitary tropical palm from a small area along Brazil's Atlantic coast. The clean trunk can be 50 feet (15m) tall and 12 inches (30cm) in diameter. It grows at low level usually not far from the coast in rainforest, and the long, pinnate, somewhat plumose leaves are carried erect. The fibers these produce are used locally for brushes, brooms, and for thatching huts and were at one time exported to Europe. The fruits are massive, up to 6 inches (15cm) long, and are borne on huge bunches which hang down from among the leaves.

Cultivation

Totally underused in cultivation, care should be taken when siting this large palm. Suitable for tropical parks and large gardens, where it can best be appreciated. When young, it makes an unusual palm for the greenhouse or conservatory, though the large seeds are erratic and often slow to germinate.

Above: Brian Trollip provides scale for Attalea funifera, *semi-cultivated, Espirito Santo, Brazil.*
Right: The large fruits are up to 6 inches (15cm) long.

Attalea humilis

Features

Unusually, the trunks of this species are mostly underground, though shortly emergent stems are sometimes seen. In other respects they resemble small versions of the others in the genus, in that the large pinnate leaves are held upright. They grow to some 10 or 13 feet (3 or 4m) in height. Very common throughout their coastal forest range in southern Brazil, one becomes quite blasé about seeing them. The fruits, the size of a large hen's egg, hang down from among the leaves and drape themselves on the ground. They are pale brown when fully ripe.

Cultivation

Other palms in this genus are not much cultivated because of their great size, but this much smaller species may be more suitable for the modest tropical garden. Again, the seeds are tough to germinate, but once this has occurred, the plants grow relatively quickly.

Above: Attalea humilis *in habitat in light woodland, Rio de Janiero State, Brazil.*
Left: The large fruits lie on the ground.

Bactris ferruginea

Features

One of what may be up to a hundred species in a very diverse genus found all over South America, it is a typically spiny clumping palm with several slim canes carrying unevenly spaced pinnate leaves, which have a ruffled, plumose appearance. All parts of the palm are covered with black spines. The round fruits are ½ or ¾ inches (1 or 2cm) in diameter and black when ripe. It occurs at low altitude near the coast in central Brazil, where it can be seen in rainforest habitats.

Cultivation

This spiny palm does not have much to recommend it as a cultivated plant. It is spiny in all its parts and would mainly be of interest to collectors. The small seeds germinate easily enough if fresh and subsequent seedling growth is also quite fast. The seedlings are quite pretty when young, and would make interesting conservatory plants for a while.

Right: Bactris ferruginea, *in habitat, Minas Gerais, Brazil.*

A Pocket Guide to Palms

Bactris gasipaes
Peach palm

Features

Well known as a cultivated plant in tropical South America, and the source of the popular fruit "Chonta," it is not known in the wild. This suckering palm has trunks of up to 50 feet (15m) tall, densely ringed with spines, though these are not apparent from a distance, and the plumose leaves are also spiny. The brightly colored fruits,

which pass through green, yellow, and finally red stages are borne in pendulous bunches. A variety from Peru, cultivated since ancient times by the indians, grows without spines and the fruits have no seeds. This fast-growing palm is also culti-vated on farms as a source of "palm heart." When the main stem is harvested, others in the clump take its place.

Cultivation

The seeds germinate easily, but may take a couple of months. Useful as a tropical fruit tree in warm climates, it also has a place as an ornamental plant when young.

Left: Bactris gasipaes, *semi-cultivated, Alajuela, Costa Rica.*

Beccariophoenix madagascariensis

Window palm

Features

An extraordinary palm seriously endangered in the wild and only recently rediscovered, but rapidly finding popularity with collectors throughout the world, which may be the only way it will be saved from extinction. Originating from a few separate locations in Madagascar only, it is a big, solitary species with a height of up to 40 feet (12m) and a handsome crown of largely upright, pinnate leaves. In young plants of one form, the leaves are large, broad, and entire and have slots or "windows" in them. It prefers mountain sides and ridges where it grows in the forest. The fruits are carried among the leaves and are 1 or 1½ inches (3 or 4cm) long, oval in shape, and purple-brown when ripe.

Cultivation

Increasingly seen both in private collections and botanic gardens, there seem to be two or three forms, the most attractive having long "windows" or splits along the folds of the young leaves. The large seeds germinate without difficulty and seedling growth is moderate.

Above: A juvenile Beccariophoenix madagascariensis, *Garrin Fullington Garden, Paradise Park, Hawaii.*

Left: The "windows" in the leaves are clearly seen here.

Bismarckia nobilis
Bismarck palm

Features

Stunningly beautiful, large, solitary palm tree, with big fan leaves that can range from green through blue to almost white-silver. From Madagascar, where it occurs in open country and savannah, it grows to around 70 feet (20m) in height and is said to be the most common palm in that country. The oval fruits, which hang down from among the leaves, are 1½ to 2 inches (4 to 4.5cm) long and brown when ripe.

Cultivation

Increasingly popular as a tropical or subtropical ornamental, it is a common sight in, say, Florida, where it is widely used in parks and gardens. Hopefully, in a few years time, other countries will wake up to its qualities as it will surely grow almost anywhere *Washingtonia* will grow. The seeds, about 1 inch (3cm) long, are easy to germinate and in good conditions young seedlings are quite fast growing. The first leaves to appear are a distinctive greeny-mauve shade, and strap shaped. It is a year or two before it begins to produce the first fan-shaped leaves.

Right: Bismarckia nobilis, *cultivated, Montgomery Botanical Center, Florida.*

Borassodendron machadonis

Features

An unusual and rare Malaysian rainforest palm with a tall, slim trunk covered with old leaf bases. Its distinctive fan-shaped leaves are broad, widely spaced, with finger-like segments and beautiful yellow and green longitudinal stripes on the petiole, which is without spines but has sharp edges. This palm is much more likely to be seen in botanic gardens than in the wild where it is under threat from collection for palm "cabbage." The big, up to 6 inches (15cm), round fruits are reddish brown when ripe and usually contain two seeds, which together form a sphere.

Cultivation

The large, hard seeds germinate quickly, given suitable conditions of warmth and humidity. Although more suitable for the tropical park or garden, it can be grown as a houseplant for a number of years. As the seeds put down long roots, a deep container should be chosen, or they should be planted in their permanent position in the ground.

Above: Borassodendron machadonis, *cultivated, Fairchild Tropical Garden, Florida.*
Right: The old leaf bases form an attractive pattern.

A Pocket Guide to Palms

Borassus aethiopum
African Palmyra palm

Features

A large, solitary, sometimes bulging, stout African palm, up to 100 feet (30m), with big, costapalmate fan-shaped leaves which leave their split bases for a while until they, too, drop off leaving the trunk bare. Growing in dry and very dry locations, such as savanna and open woodland, they have a number of local uses and populations are dying out for this reason. The big fruits, about 4 inches (10cm) in diameter, are produced among the leaves.

Cultivation

The seeds germinate easily and quickly if given a good soak, and produce a long "sinker" best accommodated in a deep pot, or direct in its permanent position in the ground. This fleshy root is appreciated as a vegetable delicacy in areas where this palm occurs naturally and consequently there is little or no regeneration of the populations.

Above: Borassus aethiopum, *semi-cultivated, Kosti, Sudan.*

Left: The large fruits can be seen among the leaves.

Borassus flabellifer
Palmyra palm

Features
Widespread palm found from India through Malaysia to Indonesia. It is a tall, solitary fan palm, with a bare trunk and blue-green, costapalmate leaves in a distinctive, spherical crown. Locally it is important economically; the cut flower stalks yield sap, which is turned into palm sugar or fermented into toddy, the timber is used for construction and the very large fruit, 6 or 8 inches (15 or 20cm) in diameter and containing three seeds, is edible. In some areas these palms grow in large colonies, which stretch as far as the eye can see, and prefer a drier, savanna location.

Cultivation
Fresh seeds germinate easily and sometimes very quickly. The long root quickly grows downwards to reach water as soon as possible, after which growth slows down somewhat. This palm makes an interesting ornamental in the tropical garden and is an attractive house or conservatory plant when young.

Left: Borassus flabellifer, *semi-cultivated, Rangoon-Moulmein road, Burma.*

A Pocket Guide to Palms

Brahea armata
Blue Hesper palm, Mexican blue palm

Features

Well-known and popular garden palm from northwestern Mexico, where it grows in dry, rocky soils, sometimes on cliff faces, sometimes in the company of *Washingtonia* palms. Its most distinctive characteristic is its big fan-shaped silvery blue leaves, though these are often more noticeable in cultivated than wild plants. It grows quite tall, up to maybe 50 feet (15m), with a thick, bare trunk. The leaf petioles are lined with thorns, and the fruits, which form on long inflorescences that arch out way beyond the leaves, are yellow to dark brown when ripe.

Cultivation

Fresh seeds germinate easily, old seeds take longer, though as desert plants, they have a long viability. They should be soaked well before sowing. Young plants grow rather slowly and it may be a few years before they develop their first fan leaves. Popular in cooler climates where when mature it can take considerable frost.

Above: The long inflorescences of Brahea armata *reach almost to the ground.*

Right: B. armata *with* Washingtonia *palms in habitat, Sonora, Mexico.*

Brahea brandegeei
San Jose Hesper palm

Features

Attractive fan palm sharing territory with *B. armata* in Mexico, though at perhaps higher elevations, even on mountains. The trunk grows to about 30 to 40 feet (10 to 12m) and is slimmer, the leaves are green with a distinctive bluish cast, especially underneath, and the petioles are thorny. The flower stalks are the same length as the leaves and the round fruits, up to ¾ inch (2cm) in diameter, are brown and glossy when ripe. They are much less common in the wild than *B. armata* and some off-road exploration may be needed to find them.

Cultivation

The seeds should be soaked for a few days before planting and will germinate in a few weeks. The young seedlings should be potted up into a sandy mix and kept barely moist. Growth is slow for the first few months or years, but gradually speeds up.

Right: Brahea brandegeei *in habitat, Sonora, Mexico.*

A Pocket Guide to Palms

Brahea decumbens

Mexican dwarf blue palm

Features

An unusual, low growing *Brahea*, unique in the genus (of about ten species). The multiple trunks are prostrate and tend to creep along the ground, where they may attain a length of 6½ or 10 feet (2 or 3m). The leaves are an attractive silver-blue. They occur in arid, rocky soils in northeast Mexico and sometimes cover huge areas. These palms grow at relatively high altitudes, which indicates their cold hardiness, though their rarity in cultivation means they have not been much tried in temperate areas. The seed is carried near the ground and often seems to be predated by insects and beetles.

Cultivation

Seeds are slowly becoming more widely available and it is hoped that before long

this pretty, small palm will be more frequently seen. It makes an excellent specimen for the arid garden and is equally suitable for a hot and dry conservatory.

Above: A handsome cultivated specimen at Huntington Botanical Gardens, California.
Left: Unripe fruits.

Brahea dulcis
Rock palm

Features

The name for this palm seems to be used for any species not clearly assignable elsewhere. It can have solitary or multiple trunks, which are thick or thin, be blue- or green-leaved, grow tall or short, and apparently covers a very wide distribution area through Mexico, right down to Central America. It should be more widely grown as it is an attractive palm in all its many forms, especially with blue leaves. Over time it may be proved that several species are included under the one name and perhaps cross pollination also plays a part in blurring the edges.

Cultivation

The seeds are oval, about ½ inch (1cm) long and should be sown fresh, after a good soaking. As with the other species, subsequent growth is rather slow.

Above: Brahea dulcis *in habitat, Tamaulipas, Mexico.*
Left: Palms are shown here growing by the thousand.

Brahea edulis
Guadalupe palm

Features

A very distinctive and unmistakable *Brahea* with big, green, roughly diamond-shaped leaves, practically extinct on its native island of Guadalupe, off the west coast of Mexico. It was the habit of early sailors to leave goats on islands to ensure a supply of fresh meat on subsequent visits. This had an often disastrous effect on the native flora and never worse than in this case. Happily it is quite common in cultivation and is often seen in botanic and private gardens in countries with subtropi-

cal to temperate climates. The round fruits are produced in huge quantities and germination is usually quite good, though erratic. Hopefully one day the island will be repopulated from cultivated plants, though who knows, maybe the pollinator will also die out in the meantime.

Cultivation

Showing some potential as a cold hardy palm, it is becoming increasingly popular, and given good conditions it is quite fast growing. Though it will tolerate frosts, it grows best in a dry, warm climate.

Left: Brahea edulis, *cultivated, Villa Thuret, Cap Ferat, France.*

Butia archeri
Dwarf jelly palm

Features

A choice though diminutive *Butia* from southeast
Brazil where it grows in just a few locations, in
loose colonies, sometimes visible from the road, in
open grassland. The thick and stubby, solitary
trunk is no more than 3 feet (1m) or so tall (sometimes subterranean) and frequently shows damage
from grass fires. The blue-green leaves, with
leaflets held in a stiff V-shape, are pinnate and
curve over in a distinctive fashion. The fruits which
are about ¾ inch (2cm) long and oval, are carried
among the leaves and are brown when ripe.

Cultivation

This would make a delightful specimen for the temperate garden, if seeds were
more readily available and easier to germinate. At the moment it is seen in just a
very few private collections. It is slow growing and takes years to form a trunk, so
much patience is required.

*Above: Trunks are frequently
burned by grass fires.
Left:* Butia archeri, *in habitat,
Minas Gerais, Brazil.*

Butia capitata
Jelly palm

Features

Well-known and distinctive hardy palm from wide areas of southeastern Brazil, where it grows in open grassland and savanna. The solitary trunk is thick and covered with the stubs of old leaf bases, sometimes in a spiral pattern. It grows to about 20 feet (6m) tall or more and supports a crown of blue-green to green recurved, pinnate leaves. The fruits, which contain a sweet yellow flesh from which jam or jelly can be made, are produced in large numbers and can also be eaten straight from the tree. The variety "Strictior" has upright leaves.

Cultivation

The seeds germinate easily given heat, humidity, and a few months. Seedling growth is comparatively fast though it may be two or three years before the first feather leaves appear. Popular as a garden palm, it can stand several degrees of frost when mature.

Above: Butia capitata in cleared pasture, Rio Grande do Sul, Brazil.
Right: "Strictior" with upright leaves, south of France.

Butia eriospatha
Woolly butia

Features

A similar palm in general appearance to *B. capitata* that grows in a slightly overlapping range in south-east Brazil, though at different altitudes. This attractive species can be distinguished by the spathe, which is covered in dense pale brown woolly tomentum, making it unmistakable. It grows in open land and savanna and can be the dominant feature of the landscape. The thick trunk grows to 16 or 20 feet (5 or 6m) tall and is covered with the bases of dead leaves giving it a rough appearance. The blue-green leaves arch attractively. The fruits, yellow when ripe, hang down from among the leaves.

Cultivation

Butia seeds should not be sown fresh and they have long viability. They should be stored cool and dry for a few months before sowing. Warmth and moisture are then required for them to germinate successfully, which they do in a few weeks. The seedlings should be transferred into a sandy mix and moved to a bright position. Keep the soil barely moist and pot on as required.

Above: Butia eriospatha *in cleared pasture, Santa Caterina, Brazil.*
Left: The woolly spathe distinguishes this species.

Butia yatay
Yatay palm

Features

This is a very common palm seen across huge areas of northern Argentina and southern Brazil, and probably numbered in hundreds of thousands. One can drive for mile after mile and see little else. Even so, this palm is being destroyed on a grand scale for pasture. A tall species, it can grow to 30 feet (10m) or more and is topped by a recurved crown of blue-green leaves. The fruits are yellow when ripe and contain a sweet flesh.

Cultivation

Thousands of trees are dug annually, ostensibly to save them from destruction, and exported by the container load to Europe where they grace the gardens of the well-heeled. This can be a successful process though they may take some years to fully recover. From seed, they are as slow-growing as their cousins. Rather hardy to frost, they can be cultivated in climatic zones from subtropical to temperate.

Left: Butia yatay *in habitat, Corrientes, Argentina, with the author.*

Calamus erectus
Viagra palm

Features

Calamus is the largest palm genus and contains around 400 species. Most are spiny, climbing palms, the source of rattan for furniture, and some have great economic importance across the tropics where they occur. *C. erectus* is an attractive northeast Indian species found growing in forest clearings in the foothills of the Himalayas. It is not a true climber, but may support itself by "leaning" against other vegetation. It grows to perhaps 15 feet (5m) tall, and the clustering stems are covered with spines. As with the others in the genus, the small pale brown fruits are covered with overlapping scales.

Cultivation

If fresh the small seeds germinate readily and easily, and the seedlings grow quite fast. They are pretty as young plants and are quite suitable as potted palms before they get too big, though they do need atmospheric humidity to prosper. The seeds lose their viability very quickly so cannot be stored.

Above: Calamus erectus, *in habitat, Teesta Valley, West Bengal, India.*
Left: The small fruits are covered in overlapping scales.

Calamus gracilis

Features

From the beautiful Khasia Hills in Meghalaya Province in northern India, this species climbs high into the tree tops, supported by other vegetation, and using hooks and spines on its specially modified leaves, hoists itself up to emerge through the forest canopy and into the light. It is a very pretty species with the leaflets arranged in groups along the rachis and makes an interesting houseplant while young. These palms look very attractive from a distance, but are very difficult, and painful, to make a path through on forest walks.

Cultivation

The small seeds lose their viability very quickly and should be sown fresh in a light, open, spongy soil mix that is kept moist and warm. They should germinate within a few weeks and the young seedlings grow rather quickly. Avoid keeping them in direct sunlight as this could burn the young leaves.

Above and left: Calamus gracilis, *in habitat, Khasia Hills, Meghalaya Province, India. The leaf grouping shows well in silhouette.*

Carpentaria acuminata
Carpentaria palm

Features

An Australian palm, easily recognized by its recurving feathery leaves and its bright red fruit. From the north of the country it is rapidly gaining popularity as a street tree because of its neat appearance and fast growth. In habitat, it grows in rainforests near streams and this gives a hint of its requirements in cultivation. It is a solitary palm, to about 30 feet (10m), with a slim trunk, and the clusters of fruit hang down from below the leaves.

Cultivation

The carmine red fruits contain seeds which germinate rather quickly though, as always, they should be sown as fresh as possible. A loose, open mix should be used, which will allow both air and moisture to reach the seeds. Once sprouted, the young plants should be potted individually and moved to brighter, though not direct, light. They grow quickly and should be potted on as necessary.

Above: Carpentaria acuminata, *cultivated, Florida.*
Left: Clusters of red fruits hang down below the leaves.

Carpoxylon macrospermum

Features

A rare and exciting palm from Vanuatu in the New Hebrides group of islands, lost to science for many years but recently rediscovered and slowly being introduced to cultivation thanks to the efforts of the local population. It is a solitary palm, with a slim trunk to about 70 feet (20m) supporting a handsome crown of long feather leaves and large, egg-sized fruits that are red when ripe. This species is a real success story. Snatched from obscurity and possible extinction, it is being protected by the islanders who sell the seed abroad, and put the income toward popularizing and exploiting their palm.

Cultivation

The seeds are said to germinate readily and seedling growth is extremely fast. Tropical conditions would suit this palm best with a plentiful supply of water, together with shade from the sun when young. Any special efforts to grow it will surely be amply repaid.

Left: Carpoxylon macrosperma, *semi-cultivated, Vanuatu.*

Caryota mitis
Clustering fishtail palm

Features

Well-known as a houseplant for many years, this species (one of about twelve in the genus) is one of the few that sucker. In habitat, it grows in tropical India across to Indonesia and up to the Philippines. It reaches 15–20 feet (5 or 6m) or so in height and consists of many slim upright stems each bearing bipinnate leaves that resemble fishes' tails. The fruits are produced on inflorescences from among the leaves and contain caustic crystals. They should be handled with great care.

Cultivation

The black, odd-shaped seeds should be removed from the flesh with care because of the stinging crystals. They germinate easily and subsequent growth is fast. Use a light, open compost and make sure it is kept warm and moist. As houseplants they are tolerant of low light and abuse and can happily stand in water for long periods. They are ideal in tropical and subtropical gardens because of their small size.

Right: Caryota mitis, *cultivated, Montgomery Botanical Center, Florida.*

A Pocket Guide to Palms

Caryota obtusa
Giant fishtail palm

Features

A huge and magnificent fishtail palm from India, Thailand, China, Burma, and Laos. It has a thick, ringed trunk and vast, spreading compound leaves and looks for all the world like a giant tree fern. It is a once-seen-never-forgotten palm and the biggest in the genus. In common with other fishtails, the fruits contain stinging crystals and merit careful handling. *Caryota* are monocarpic, that is, they die after flowering and fruiting. Very fast growing in conditions of warmth and humidity.

Cultivation

Palms of this size require careful siting, especially as they are not long-lived. It is suitable for a tropical park or large garden, where its awesome stature can best be appreciated. The odd-shaped seeds germinate easily and quickly if fresh and the seedlings grow very quickly, a hint of what is to come. They also make good houseplants while small, and tolerate neglect.

Left: The author gives a sense of scale to Caryota obtusa *in habitat, Khasia Hills, Meghalaya Province, India.*

Caryota maxima "Himalaya"

Himalayan fishtail palm

Features

This lovely palm with tumbling leaves with leaflets shaped like fishes' tails grows at some altitude in the foothills of the Himalayas in northeastern India where it endures quite low temperatures, even frost and snow, during the winter. For this reason it may be considered worth trying in the sheltered garden in temperate areas. It is a solitary palm, rather tall and very fast growing, with a ringed trunk that has noticeable internodes and a crown of leaves much taller than it is wide. It grows in a semi-

cultivated state across a wide area and in some places is rather common. *C. maxima* also grows across much of Southeast Asia.

Cultivation

The black seeds germinate quite easily, if fresh, and seedling growth is rather fast. In ideal conditions this palm will grow 3 to 6 feet (1 or 2m) of trunk per year. It has recently begun to be seen more frequently in palm collections and soon it will surely filter through to parks and gardens, where it will prove a welcome addition.

Left: Caryota maxima *"Himalaya," semi-cultivated, Kalimpong, W. Bengal, India.*

Ceroxylon alpinum
Andean wax palm

Features

One in a genus of about ten species, this South American palm tree is famous for the layer of wax covering the trunk. They grow at high altitudes, up to 7,000 feet (2,000m), in the Andes Mountains in the north west and are tall, solitary palms, up to about 70 feet (20m) in height, with a crown of mostly horizontally carried leaves, the leaflets of which hang down each side of the rachis. The underside of the leaves is covered with brown scurf, and the trunk appears almost white from the thin covering of wax. The small round seeds are carried in large clusters and are orange to red when ripe, and pitted.

Cultivation

The seeds germinate readily, though seedling growth is rather slow. A light, open mix, perhaps containing sphagnum moss, will increase germination rates, and the plants should be grown on in an acidic soil mix to keep them content. They are happy in cool, moist conditions though not truly cold hardy.

Above: Ceroxylon alpinum, *semi-cultivated, outside Quito, Ecuador.*
Left: Toby Spanner lends scale to a leaf of Ceroxylon sp.

Ceroxylon echinulatum
Pumbo wax palm

Features

Extremely common in some areas of its native Ecuador, this attractive species has leaflets which hang down like curtains either side of the rachis (leaf stem) and are covered on the undersides with yellow scurf. It grows to 70 feet (20m) or so tall at altitudes of up to 6,500 feet (2,000m), and the seeds, which are orangey-red when ripe and covered with blunt spines, are produced in huge numbers. The name comes from the Greek for wax (*keros*) and wood (*xylon*).

Cultivation

The small seeds germinate easily and quickly though the seedlings are rather slow growing. *Ceroxylon* palms prefer cool and moist conditions and in the wild are often surrounded with mist and cloud, an indication of their preferences in cultivation. They grow best in acid, peaty soil and take many years to form a trunk. They are happy in temperate climates though their actual cold tolerance is not great.

Left: Ceroxylon echinulatum, *in habitat, looming through the mist near Valledolid, Ecuador.*

A Pocket Guide to Palms

Ceroxylon parvifrons

Features

Quite different from most others in the genus, the leaves of *C. parvifrons* are curved and stiffly held, and the leaflets, which are covered on the under-side with yellow brown scurf, are vertical giving a unique appearance. It occurs across the northwest corner of South America and has the distinction of being among the highest altitude palms in the world, growing at up to an incredible 10,500 feet (3,200m). Often shrouded by cloud, it is an amazing sight on the chilly, misty Andes mountainsides.

Cultivation

Fresh seeds should be used as *Ceroxylon* seeds seem to lose their viability rather quickly. Planted in an open mix, they should sprout within a few weeks. Slow growing throughout all stages of growth, they enjoy cool and moist conditions out of direct sunlight. This palm seems to be the most cold hardy and tolerates temperatures down to 23 or 19 F (-5 or -7 C) when older.

Top: Ceroxylon parvifrons *in habitat, Santa Barbara, Ecuador.*
Above: Unripe fruit will eventually turn red.

Ceroxylon quinduiense
Quindio wax palm

Features

This is probably the best known *Ceroxylon* and is the national tree of its native Colombia. They grow in vast numbers and are often left when forest is cleared for pasture but any seedlings are likely to be eaten by cattle, so it is only a temporary stay of execution. The palms grow to an incredible 200 feet (60m) high and are the tallest in the world. The trunks are covered with a once commercially important white wax and the fruits, which grow to ¾ inch (2cm) in diameter, are produced in huge numbers and are orange-red and smooth when ripe.

Cultivation

As with the other species in the genus, an open soil mix with the addition of some moss will ensure the best germination; thereafter, the young plants grow frustratingly slowly to begin with but be patient, they later speed up dramatically. Because of its high altitude, this is one of the cold-hardiest species. Even so, this only develops with age.

Left: Ceroxylon quinduiense *in habitat, near El Cajon, southwest of Cajamarca, Colombia, approximately 8,200 feet (2,500m).*

Chamaedorea brachypoda

Features

Chamaedorea is a large Central American genus containing upwards of 70 species of usually small, rainforest palms many of which are well-known in cultivation because of their tolerance of low light and general neglect. *C. brachypoda* is not so well-known, which is a shame because with its simple, entire, grass-green leaves and small stature, it is a beautiful palm and would make an ideal houseplant. It grows to about 6 or 7 feet (2m) only, spreads by rhizomes and is fast growing, especially in the tropical climate it prefers. The fruits are small, round, and black when ripe. As with all in the genus, male and female flowers are on separate plants.

Cultivation

As with most of the species in the genus, it makes a pretty houseplant that tolerates low light. This, together with its ease of germination and fast growth should increase its popularity as soon as it becomes more widely available. In the tropical and subtropical garden, it makes a splendid border specimen that will soon fill its allotted space.

Right: Chamaedorea brachypoda,
cultivated, Florida.

Chamaedorea cataractarum
Cat palm

Features

A thickly clumping palm from Mexico, with dense, dark green foliage which makes it instantly recognizable. It grows to about 6 or 7 feet (2m) in height, has many slim stems in the clump and spreads rather fast given the wet and warm conditions it prefers. The small fruits are carried within the clump and are black when ripe. It has become extremely popular as a houseplant over the last few years as its qualities are recognized and as it has become more widely available.

Cultivation

The small seeds sprout soon after sowing, especially if they are fresh. Growing as it does in streams and cataracts, it is able to tolerate very damp, even wet soil, and thus scores as a houseplant for those who tend to be heavy handed with the watering can. Outside it is a great palm for the tropical garden where it fills a valuable place as an understory palm, which will happily grow in the shade of other plants.

Right: Chamaedorea cataractarum, *cultivated, Florida.*

Chamaedorea linearis

Features

A rainforest palm from the western edge of the northern half of South America, where it grows in clearings and is often visible from the road, usually at quite high altitudes. It is tall for a *Chamaedorea*, at up to 30 feet (10m), with solitary stems, ringed with old leaf scars, to about 2 or 3 inches (6 or 8cm) in diameter, and is usually seen growing up from among other foliage. The bright red fruits, up to ¾ inch (2cm) in diameter, are carried in pendulous bunches below the leaves, often the first thing to attract attention against a background of green.

Cultivation

An easy palm to grow, the round seeds germinate quickly if they are fresh, and the young plants are characterful from the outset. It makes a good interior plant for the home or conservatory; in the garden in warmer climates it is a striking small palm for the mixed border, the bright red fruits providing an additional benefit.

Left: Chamaedorea linearis, *in habitat, northern Ecuador.*

Chamaedorea metallica

Metallica palm

Features

Much loved small palm for the interior, or outside in warmer climate gardens. The simple and entire leaves are dark green with a noticeable metallic sheen, unmistakable. There is also a split leaf form in cultivation, with both leaf shapes sometimes on the same plant. The stems are solitary and up to 6 or 10 feet (2 or 3m) tall and the flowers, unusually, are orange. It grows in a small area of southern Mexico, but is widely cultivated around the world. The round fruits are about ½ inch (1cm) across and black when ripe.

Cultivation

Fresh seeds are easy to sprout, and germinate within a few weeks given warmth and humidity. The young plants are recognizable from an early age and grow quite quickly. Best planted three plants to a pot for indoor use, they tolerate low light conditions extremely well, perfect for a low-lit spot in the home.

Above: The divided leaf form.

Left: Chamaedorea metallica, cultivated, Australia.

Chamaedorea microspadix
Bamboo palm

Features

An attractive clustering rainforest palm, which occurs naturally in one small area of southern Mexico where it grows at quite high altitudes, up to 5,000 feet (1,500m). This no doubt contributes to its cold hardiness and plants have commonly withstood 18 F (-8 C) in cultivation. The stems (only about ½ inch (1cm) in diameter) grow in big clumps, to about 10 feet (3m) tall and bear small, round fruits in greens, reds, and yellows.

Cultivation

As with others in the genus, the small round seeds germinate readily if fresh, usually within a few weeks of sowing. They should be mixed with moist peat and kept somewhere warm and dark until they sprout. Transfer the plantlets to 2 inch (5cm) pots and move to a brighter spot, but out of direct sunshine. Suitable for planting out in tropical gardens or in sheltered gardens in temperate zones, where they will tolerate considerable frost.

Right: Chamaedorea microspadix, *in habitat, Hildago, Mexico.*

Chamaedorea radicalis

Features

An unusual and hardy *Chamaedorea* from high altitudes, to 3,000 feet (1,000m), in central Mexico, where it grows in oak forests. The dark green leaves look tough and leathery and the fruits are carried on upright flower stalks up to 3 feet (1m) long, which as the fruits ripen bend down under the weight almost as if to deposit the seeds as far from the parent plant as possible. The fruits themselves pass through green, yellow, and orange, finally ripening to bright red.

Cultivation

Germination is as for the other species, and is equally fast if the seeds are fresh. The leathery leaves are rather hardy to cold and can withstand 18 F (-8 C) or even colder, thus a valuable addition to the temperate garden, where they seem happiest in shade. They also make attractive house plants growing in low light in the home.

Right: Chamaedorea radicalis, *cultivated, Royal Botanic Gardens, Kew, England.*

Chamaerops humilis
Mediterranean fan palm

Features

One of the most widely used landscape palms in the world, this popular, suckering, fan-leaved, shrubby palm occurs around the western half of the Mediterranean where it grows on rocky and arid soil often in vast colonies. The stems, which are covered with old leaf bases, are no more than 3 feet (1m) or so tall (more in cultivation), the leaf stalks are lined with thorns and the ½ to ¾ inch (1 or 2cm) diameter fruits are brown-red when ripe. Many forms of this variable palm have been recorded.

Cultivation

Seeds should be cleaned of flesh and allowed to dry out for a few days. Mix with moist compost and keep in a warm or hot place and they will germinate in a few weeks. Seedling growth is quite slow. This palm is very hardy to cold and is widely used in temperate gardens where it can tolerate severe frosts when older. When young they are also happy in the hot, dry conservatory.

Above: Chamaerops humilis,
cultivated, Italy.
Left: The ripe, oily fruits are
orange to brown.

Chamaerops humilis var. cerifera

Blue Moroccan fan palm

Features

This attractive form of *Chamaerops humilis* probably deserves species status as it is markedly different from the foregoing. The fan-shaped leaves are covered with a bluish waxy coating on both surfaces, and it bears black thorns. It was described early last century by Beccari, though he did not know where it occurred in the wild. In fact it grows, often in vast colonies, in the arid Atlas Mountains of Morocco from where it was brought into general cultivation just a few years ago. It is found almost up to the snow line and is extremely hardy.

Cultivation

Germinate the seeds as for *Chamaerops humilis*, it may help to give them a good soak first. The first leaves to be produced are green; the blue comes with the adult leaves. It is a wonderful plant suitable for the garden, home, or hot, dry, and bright conservatory.

Above and left: Chamaerops humilis *var.* cerifera, *in habitat, Atlas Mountains, Morocco.*

Chambeyronia macrocarpa

Red leaf palm

Features

An exciting, recently available rainforest palm from
New Caledonia. The solitary trunk, ringed with old
leaf scars, is up to 30 feet (10m) tall and bears a
handsome crown of feather-shaped, leathery leaves, the newest of which opens
bright scarlet red, changing slowly to green. There is a prominent green crownshaft
and the large fruits, up to 2 inches (5cm) long, when ripe, are also red.

Cultivation

The large seeds are rather easy to germinate,
though they are best sown fresh. They should be
soaked if they appear dry, then mixed with moist
peat and placed in a warm spot, in the dark. They
should sprout within a few weeks. Remove the
plantlets and pot up individually. Seedling growth is
moderate though it will be some time before the
red tint of the new leaves appears. This is a wonderful palm in the warm-temperate to tropical garden, and also as a houseplant while young.

Above: Chambeyronia macrocarpa, *semi-cultivated, New
Caledonia.*
Left: The new leaf is bright red.

Chuniophoenix hainanensis

Hainan fan palm

Features

Hainan is a tropical island off the south coast of China and is the home of this beautiful palm, which grows in rainforest in low mountain ranges. It is of moderate size, only 10 or 12 feet (3 or 4m) tall at maturity and the stems sucker forming a shrubby or bushy shape. The leaves, which have spreading, finger-like leaf seg-

ments have no hastula and are almost unique in this respect. One other interesting feature is the great bunches of bright red fruits, up to ¾ inch (2cm) in diameter, which adorn the clump when ripe. It is one of only two species in the genus.

Cultivation

The round seeds germinate easily if kept in the dark in warm, moist peat for a few weeks. The seedlings grow quite fast though it will be some time before the first character leaves appear.

Left: Chuniophoenix hainanensis, *cultivated, South China Botanical Gardens, Guangzhou, China.*

Coccothrinax argentata
Silver thatch palm

Features

One of about fifteen species in the genus, it is native to extreme south Florida and the western Caribbean. It is a small, slim, solitary palm with a crown of delightful glossy green, fan-shaped leaves that have distinctive silvery backs. The leaves are seen to best effect in a gentle breeze, when the upper and lower surfaces contrast. Sometimes these palms grow in profusion, and are commonly seen on the Florida Keys, not far from the road. The trunk is only a few inches in diameter and covered, at least at the top, with a network of old leaf bases. The small round fruits are produced in generous quantities and are dark mauve when ripe.

Cultivation

The small seeds germinate readily enough, the only drawback being that the plants grow unreasonably slowly. Mature plants seen for sale are usually taken from the wild, an undesirable practice that results in the death of many plants. Full sun and a sandy soil will benefit this attractive palm's growth and the final results are definitely worth the wait.

Above: Coccothrinax argentata, cultivated, Fairchild Tropical Garden, Florida.
Left: The ripe fruits are purple.
Far left: The leaf back is silvery white.

Coccothrinax barbadensis
Silver palm

Features

Once common on many Caribbean Islands, the range of this palm is now much reduced due to the ravages of the domestic goat. On Antigua for example, it is almost extinct. Bizarrely, the only trees still living there are confined to the cathedral cemetery which is fenced off, some growing from broken tombs. It is a tall and slim palm, its solitary trunk just 3 or 4 inches (3cm) or so in diameter, and up to 50 feet (15m) in height. It is naked along its length with but a few fibers and old leaf bases at the top. The leaves are fan-shaped, glossy green above, silvery below, and the small round fruits are purple to black when ripe.

Cultivation

The small round seeds germinate quickly in warmth in a sandy soil, but are very slow thereafter. The first leaves are grass-like and it will be a number of years before character leaves are produced.

Right: Coccothrinax barbadensis *growing in the cathedral cemetary, Antigua.*

Coccothrinax crinita
Old Man palm

Features

The most easily recognized in the genus, the slim trunk is covered with a thick layer of long hair-like brown fibers making it look much thicker than it actually is. In much older plants, this fiber is lost at the bottom of the trunk. The leaves are fan-shaped and rather stiff, dull green above and silvery gray below. The Old Man palm pro-

duces quantities of round seed fruits about ½ inch (1cm) in diameter, which are black when ripe. It is now all but extinct in the wild in its native Cuba, but happily rather common in cultivation throughout the tropics where it will have to survive.

Cultivation

Much patience is required to grow these attractive palms. The seeds germinate easily but subsequent growth is very slow, taking some years for the early grass-like leaves to be replaced by adult ones. However, the unusual trunk fibers are seen from an early age, adding to the interest.

Left: Coccothrinax crinita, *cultivated, Fairchild Tropical Garden, Florida.*

Coccothrinax miraguama
Miraguama palm

Features
This stiff-leaved *Coccothrinax* has many variations and many names, most of which are probably invalid. It occurs in open woodland in Cuba, has a slim trunk up to 50 feet (15m) in height, and an open crown of small, fan-shaped leaves with stiff segments, giving a unique silhouette. The upper surface is green, the lower silvery. The trunk is usually covered with net-like persistent threads, which look almost like woven fabric. The small round fruits are purple to black (there is a form with rose-pink fruits) when ripe. Altogether a beautiful palm.

Cultivation
As with the other species, unreasonably slow growth is often a bar to cultivating these pretty palms. The small seeds sprout quickly, the first leaves are grass-like, but take some years to begin to produce the characteristic fan-shaped leaves of the adult plant.

Left: Coccothrinax miraguama, *cultivated,*
Fairchild Tropical Garden, Florida.

Cocos nucifera
Coconut palm

Features

The precise origin of this quintessentially tropical palm is unknown, but it grows along the shoreline, (and sometimes inland) of most tropical countries and has been cultivated for its many uses, for centuries. It can be tall, up to 60 or 70 feet (20m) in height, with a solitary, ringed trunk that has an attractive crown of large, yellow-green feather shaped leaves which wave seductively in the breeze. The fruit is the familiar coconut with a thick outer coat to make it both resistant to damage (it has a long way to fall) and buoyant, so that it may float off to distant shores.

Cultivation

The coconut should be planted entire, half buried in a growing medium of mixed sand and peat, kept moist. After some weeks or months, roots should appear from the underside of the fruit, followed by the leaves which emerge from one of the three pores in the end of the seed. Sometimes seen for sale in supermarkets and plant shops, they make interesting houseplants for a few months or years, but need humidity and bright light to succeed.

Above: Cocos nucifera, *leans seaward in characteristic fashion, Seychelles.*

Left: Coconut palms are cultivated by the thousand for home use.

Copernicia alba

Caranday palm

Features

Surely one of the most numerous palms in the world, one can drive for hour after hour in Argentina and see little else. It also occurs in adjacent Brazil, Paraguay and Bolivia, where its cut trunks are frequently used as telegraph poles. It grows to about 80 feet (25m) tall, is solitary, and has a handsome crown of blue-green, waxy, fan-shaped leaves with silvery undersides. These palms grow in dry savanna though sometimes they may be inundated for weeks at a time during periods of flooding. The fruits are oval, about ¾ by ½ inch (2 by 1cm), black and shiny when ripe.

Cultivation

The oval seeds sprout without difficulty in a few weeks in moist peat. Seedling growth is rather slow to begin with, but speeds up as the plant gets older. There is no apparent explanation as to why this palm, so common in the wild and so generous with seed, is so rare as to be almost non-existent in cultivation.

Right: Copernicia alba *in habitat, flooded grassland, Formosa, Argentina.*

Copernicia baileyana

Bailey's palm

Features

A "once-seen-never-forgotten" palm with a huge and sometimes swollen, smooth, pale gray trunk and a large, handsome crown of circular, stiff, fan-shaped, blue-green leaves looking quite stunning against the azure sky of its native central Cuba. They grow to about 60 or 70 feet tall (20m) and the trunk can be up to 24 inches (60cm) in diameter, a monster of the palm world. The round fruits are nearly an inch (3cm) in diameter, are black when ripe, and are carried on long fruit stalks that hang out well beyond the leaves.

Cultivation

As may be imagined these huge trees are not fast growing, and even small plants may be many years old. However, growers with an eye to the future are producing them in good numbers and they are increasingly available at palm nurseries, where, under-standably, they fetch a high price. From seed, they take many years to form a trunk.

Left: Copernicia baileyana, *cultivated, Fairchild Tropical Garden, Florida.*

Copernicia hospita

Features

Another handsome *Copernicia*, native to Cuba, with, in cultivation at least, silver-blue leaves. It is much smaller than *Copernicia baileyana* and rarely exceeds 20 or 25 feet (7 or 8m) in height. The leaves are circular in outline, quite stiff with many segments, and covered with a waxy layer on both surfaces. The fruits are around ¾ inches (2 cm) in diameter, round or oval, and black when ripe. This palm has several local uses, which include using the trunks for building, and making hats and baskets from the leaves.

Cultivation

The round seeds germinate in two to three months in a moist peaty mix that is kept warm. Seedlings grow quite slowly and should be potted on as required. They require bright light, an adequate supply of water, and full sun in the tropical garden.

Above: Copernicia hospita, cultivated, Fairchild Tropical Garden.
Far left: Note the long inflorescences.
Left: Stunning blue leaves of a young plant.

Copernicia macroglossa
Cuban petticoat palm

Features

Unique and easily recognized palm with a dense skirt of dead leaves, which stay on the trunk for many years giving an extraordinary effect. The stiff leaves are fan-shaped, circular in outline, green above, and silvery beneath. Growing to about 15 or 20 feet (5 or 6m) in height this palm is a native of the Cuban savanna where the cut trunks are used by the locals for fence posts. The round fruits are around ¾ inches (2 cm) in diameter and are carried on flower stalks which extend beyond the leaves. They are black when ripe.

Cultivation

An unusual addition to the tropical garden, this palm, alas, takes many years to assume its characteristic shape and much patience would be required to grow it from seed. Small plants are fortunately becoming more widely available from specialist palm nurseries, though they carry a high price tag.

Right: Copernicia macroglossa, *cultivated, Caracas Botanic Garden, Venezuela.*

Corypha umbraculifera
Talipot palm

Features

A huge palm, to some 80 feet (25m) in height, with massive, fan shaped leaves which can be 10 or 15 feet (4 or 5m) in diameter each capable, it is said, of sheltering ten men from the rain! Taking up to 50 years to flower, the tree dies after fruiting. It is native to India and Sri Lanka, where its spectacular and enormous terminal inflorescence is a stunning sight. After flowering, the round fruits, about 1½ inches (4cm) in diameter, are produced in huge numbers. Many local uses are recorded for this famous palm.

Cultivation

This massive palm needs careful siting in view of its ultimate size. A tropical park or large garden would be the ideal place where it could best be appreciated. The round seeds germinate rather easily if fresh, and the young plants also grow at a reasonable speed.

Above: Corypha umbraculifera, cultivated, Caracas Botanic Garden, Venezuela.
Left: The largest flowering structure in the world. It contains millions of individual flowers.

Corypha utan
Gebang palm

Features

A huge palm, one in a genus of about eight species, native from India through south and east Asia to Australia. In the wild it forms large colonies, in cultivation it is a spectacular addition to the tropical park or garden, where its great size can best be appreciated. It grows to about 65 feet (20m) in height. The huge flowering structure (largest in the vegetable kingdom) contains millions of creamy-white flowers, the fruits are the size of golf balls and rain down in great numbers when ripe. The tree dies after fruiting.

Cultivation

Suitable only for the park or large garden, this tropical palm requires lots of space to grow and to be seen. The seeds germinate within a few weeks of sowing if they are fresh. Seedling growth is quite fast.

Above: Corypha utan, cultivated, Caracas
  Botanic Garden, Venezuela.
Right: After flowering and fruiting, the tree
  will die.

Cryosophila nana
Rootspine palm

Features
One of a genus of about nine species, this small, pretty palm grows to no more than 15 feet (5m) in height and carries a neat crown of circular, fan-shaped leaves. However, it is the trunk which is of greater interest as it is covered in spines which in fact are undeveloped roots. They can be quite sharp and are probably a defense against browsing animals. It occurs all along the southern and western coast of Mexico and is sometimes conserved when forests are cut for pasture though whether it reproduces under these conditions is doubtful. The round fruits are about ¾ inches (1.5cm) in diameter and white when ripe.

Cultivation
The round seeds germinate easily within a few weeks if fresh, but the seedlings grow slowly. Despite the name (*Cryosophila* means "frost loving") they seem to be rather sensitive to cold and would probably do best in the tropics or sub-tropics.

Above: Cryosophila nana, *in
    cleared pasture, Pochutla,
    Oaxaca, Mexico.*
*Right: The fruits will turn from
    green to white as they ripen.*
*Far right: Roots modified into
    spines give the Rootspine palm
    its common name.*

Cyrtostachys renda
Sealing wax or Maharajah palm

Features

This unmistakable and much sought-after tropical palm from swampy coastal areas in Thailand and Malaysia has bright, sealing wax red petioles and leaf bases, which together with the neat appearance and dark green of the feather-shaped leaves makes for a delightful and attractive plant. The narrow trunks sucker, and grow to about 15 feet (5m) in height; the small oval fruits are black when ripe. A popular ornamental in Southeast Asia, cultivated plants grace many a doorway and garden.

Cultivation

The small seeds have a very short period of viability so should be planted without delay. Choose a peaty soil mix, kept damp and warm. Germination is quite fast though the subsequent seedlings grow very slowly and it takes some time before the red is first seen. Extremely sensitive to cold, Sealing wax palm is only suitable for the tropics or, in cooler climates, the hot and humid glasshouse.

Right: Cyrtostachys renda, *cultivated, Johor Baharu, Malaysia.*

Daemonorrhops jenkinsiana

Major Jenkins' rattan palm

Features

"Unfriendly" would be the best way to describe this climbing palm which is covered in all its parts with spines. A native of north eastern India, Bhutan, Bangladesh, and Burma, where it grows at low elevations, it has slim stems, which scramble up into the forest canopy, aided by backward facing hooks and spines. The leaves are finely pinnate and quite pretty especially when young though they too are extremely spiny. The fruits are attractive also, covered with tiny overlapping scales, and are yellow-brown when ripe.

Cultivation

The small round seeds germinate easily and quickly if fresh, and the young plants make appealing house palms while young, though their fierce armament may put many people off growing them. In the tropical or subtropical garden, they require a position near trees which they will use to support themselves on their journey up into the light.

Above: Daemonorrhops jenkinsiana, in habitat, W. Bengal, India.
Left: This inflorescence is about to open.

Desmoncus orthacanthus

Features

A spiny, climbing palm, widespread throughout the upper half of South America where it clambers up into the tree tops, assisted by an extension of the rachis (the cirrus), which has the leaves modified into much reduced, backward facing hooks. The feather leaves have a distinctive, prominent central vein in the leaflet, a further aid to recognition. The suckering, spine-covered stems are slim and up to 40 feet (12m) long, and the pretty fruits, about ¾ inch (2cm) long, are yellow or orange-red when ripe. These palms are more common than may be realized since much of the plant is usually hidden in the surrounding vegetation and is only visible when it emerges from the canopy.

Cultivation

The round seeds germinate easily but need to be quite fresh. The young plants grow very quickly and have very long internodes which enable them to take advantage of newly created light gaps in the forest.

Above: Desmoncus orthacanthus, *in habitat, Espirito Santo, Brazil.*
Right: The leaf tip is modified for climbing.

Dictyocaryum lamarckianum
Barrigona palm

Features

A stunningly beautiful large palm from the western edge of the top half of South America where it grows—often in big colonies—on forested slopes of the Andes Mountains in areas of high rainfall. It has a solitary, sometimes swollen, white to grey trunk up to 80 feet (25m) tall, a prominent crownshaft and just a few huge, upright, densely plumose leaves like giant bottle brushes. The erect inflorescences appear below the crownshaft and the round fruits are up to 1 inch (3cm) in diameter, and yellow-green when ripe. The first sight of this amazing palm is never forgotten.

Cultivation

The large seeds germinate easily and quickly and subsequent seedling growth is also rather fast. These palms require conditions of high humidity and high rainfall and though they grow in great profusion in the wild they are not often seen in cultivation, an indication perhaps of their precise requirements.

Left: Dictyocaryum lamarckianum, *in habitat, Ecuador.*

Dictyosperma album
Hurricane or Princess palm

Features

An attractive and widely grown palm with a ringed, grey trunk which tapers up from the enlarged base in a distinctive fashion. The leaves are feather shaped and the tips of the leaflets are often joined together by persistent "reins." It grows to around 15 to 20 feet (5 to 6m) in height and is now rare in its native Mascarene Islands where it has been much reduced by collection for palm "cabbage." The flowers are fragrant and followed by large numbers of dark red to black, oval fruits to ¾ inch (1.5cm) long.

Cultivation

Easily grown from seed, the Hurricane palm makes a good indoor subject tolerating low light and neglect. Fresh seeds should be planted in moist peat and kept warm. They will sprout in a few weeks. Ideal too for the tropical or subtropical garden, it grows best in a sunny position with adequate ground water.

Right: Dictyosperma album, *cultivated, Fairchild Tropical Garden, Florida.*

Dypsis decaryi
Triangle palm

Features

Previously known as *Neodypsis decaryi*, this distinctive Madagascan palm is endangered in habitat, but fortunately it is widely cultivated. It is easily recognized by the trunk, up to about 25 feet (7 or 8m) tall, often covered at the top with reddish brown velvet-like tomentum, and the three ranks of leaves which radiate outward from it. The inflorescence with many branches appears from among the leaf bases and bears oval fruits about ½ inch (1cm) long, brown when ripe. With its unusual shape and the formation of its silvery leaves, it makes a valuable addition to the tropical garden.

Cultivation

The oval seeds germinate readily and seedling growth is quite fast. Sow them in moist peat and keep this warm. They should sprout in a few weeks. Pot on seedlings as required and keep in bright but indirect light. Outdoors these attractive and unusual palms prefer full sun and are rather drought tolerant.

Above and left: Dypsis decaryi,
   cultivated, Marriott Beach Resort,
   Kauai, Hawaii.

Dypsis decipiens
Manambe palm

Features

A tough and hardy palm from Madagascar, previously known as *Chrysalidocarpus decipiens*. It is slowly gaining popularity as it is more widely available and it is now not uncommonly seen in collections. It is a big palm, up to 65 feet (20m) tall, with a swollen, ringed trunk, a crownshaft, and a handsome crown of glaucous green feather-shaped leaves, recurved and with the leaflets pointing upward in a distinctive fashion. The flower stalks bearing yellow flowers appear below the crownshaft and produce round fruits about ¾ inch (2cm) in diameter.

Above: Dypsis decipiens, *cultivated, Lakeside Palmetum, Oakland, CA, USA.*

Cultivation

The round seeds germinate in about eight weeks in conditions of moisture and warmth. The resulting plants grow rather slowly but steadily, and the first leaves are already rather stiff. Ideal for subtropical gardens with good rainfall, there is some evidence that this palm is hardy to cold, though full hardiness would only be attained with age.

Dypsis lutescens
Butterfly or Golden cane palm

Features

Probably the most popular indoor palm in the world, it is grown by the hundreds of thousands for sale in chainstores. From Madagascar, it is a clustering species formerly known as *Chrysalidocarpus lutescens*. The slim stems, up to 25 feet (7 or 8m) tall, are prominently ringed and carry long, arching, feather-shaped leaves with sterns golden in sunlight. The bunches of fruits, which when ripe are yellow, are produced among the leaves in large quantities. The seeds are sold commercially by the million.

Cultivation

An easily grown garden palm in tropical or subtropical locations, it grows fast and may have to be trimmed from time to time. The small seeds germinate readily and are usually planted several to a pot. In the home it requires bright light and certainly benefits from humidity in the air. It does not like the cold.

Right: Dypsis lutescens, *cultivated, Johor Baharu, Malaysia.*

A Pocket Guide to Palms

Elaeis guineensis
African oil palm

Features

A rather untidy palm, up to 65 feet (20m) in height, with a crown of somewhat plumose feather-shaped leaves, and red to black fruits. It is grown by the million for the edible oil produced from the fruits and seeds. Vast areas of the tropics are covered with plantations of these palms to the detriment of the natural flora. In some areas, one can drive for hours and miles seeing little else but oil palm plantations. Special long handled chisel-like knives are used to cut loose the bunches of fruits which are then trucked to nearby factories where the oil is extracted by crushing and boiling. It is a hugely important commercial crop.

Cultivation

The seeds, ¾ inch (2cm) round with a pointed end, are as hard as stones and not easy to germinate. They require very warm conditions and a moist, peaty substrate.

Once sprouted the young seedlings are quite pretty and may be used as houseplants for a few years. In the tropical garden they are sometimes planted as an ornament.

Above: Elaeis guineensis, cultivated, Montgomery Botanical Center.

Left: The shiny black fruits are densely packed.

Elaeis oleifera

American oil palm

Features

Frequently seen wild, cultivated, or semi-cultivated in swampy areas in Central America and the north of South America, this close relative of *Elaeis guineensis* has a trunk to 20 feet (6m) tall, often creeping along the ground for some of its length, arching leaves with leaflets held flat, and yellow to red fruits, up to 1 inch (3cm) long. It is used locally for oil production but nothing like to the extent of its African cousin. It is quite a big palm and the trunk is covered with old leaf bases. The

bunches of fruit are produced half buried between the leaves and it is not an easy job to extract them, requiring skill and a sharp knife.

Cultivation

The hard seeds are difficult to germinate and may respond to filing or soaking, even so they may require some months to sprout. Young plants can be used in the home and the trees make attractive although large subjects for the tropical garden.

Left: Elaeis oleifera, *semi-cultivated, Minas Gerais, Brazil.*

Euterpe edulis
Juçara palm

Features

Beautiful and delicate-looking tropical palm from coastal southern Brazil where it grows in small colonies across a wide area. The slim, solitary trunk, to about 30 feet (10m) tall, supports a crown of finely feathered leaves. A group of these palms makes a fine site against a Brazilian sunset. The small fruits are round and about ½ inch (1cm) across and black when ripe. They are produced in large numbers on inflorescences which appear below the crown shaft.

Cultivation

The small seeds germinate easily and quickly if fresh. If not planted soon after harvesting they may take much longer, or not grow at all. Young plants are often grouped several to a pot and sold as houseplants, as which they are well suited. As exterior plants they seem to require special conditions and are not often seen away from their native South America, where they are grown commercially for "heart of palm."

Right: Euterpe edulis, *in habitat, Espirito Santo, Brazil.*

Euterpe precatoria

Features

Beautiful slim solitary palm, which grows across most of the top half of South America, sometimes at low elevations along river banks, sometimes in wet forests at elevations of up to 6,500 feet (2,000m), which suggests that it may be more cold-tolerant than some of the other six or seven species in the genus. The trunk, which can grow to 65 feet (20m) tall, has a diameter of just a few inches and the leaves, which are pendulous, hang down in a characteristic fashion, either side of the rachis. The inflorescences grow below the crownshaft and the fruits, which are produced in large numbers, are a dark purple when ripe.

Cultivation

The small round seeds should be planted when fresh, and mixed with moist peat and kept warm. Under these conditions they should germinate within a few weeks. The young seedlings grow quickly also, and make good houseplants. Not often seen away from home they seem difficult as garden subjects.

Right: Euterpe precatoria, *in habitat, Valledolid, Ecuador.*

Gastrococos crispa
Cuban belly palm

Features

An extraordinary palm from Cuba with a noticeable swelling at the mid point of the trunk. It grows to about 50 feet (15m) tall and has a handsome crown of slightly plumose, spiny, feather-shaped leaves that are green above and silvery beneath. When young this palm is rather spiny and unfriendly, but it loses some of its armament with age. It is commonly seen semi-cultivated all around Havana and in the Cuban countryside and is often conserved by farmers. The showy flowers are yellow and the round fruits, about ¾–1 inch (2–3cm) in diameter, are bright orange when ripe.

Cultivation

The hard seeds are not easy to germinate and several techniques have been used to speed up the process. These include filing and soaking in dilute acid. Once sprouted the seedlings grow slowly though faster with age. Tropical conditions suit it best.

Left: Gastrococos crispa*, cultivated, Montgomery Botanical Center, Florida.*

Geonoma interrupta
Caña brava

Features
One of a large genus of some fifty species. They are usually small and extremely pretty palms of the South American rainforest, not much used in cultivation, which is a pity. Caña brava grows in a narrow band in the northwest of the continent often on forested slopes in areas of high rainfall. It is a small palm with a slim, ringed trunk to just a few inches in diameter and up to 20 feet (7m) tall with a crown of broadly pinnate leaves that have large and unevenly shaped leaflets. The flowering stems appear below the crownshaft and carry fruits about ½ inch (1cm) in diameter, which are black when ripe.

Cultivation
The small round seeds germinate easily and quickly. The characterful young plants grow quite fast too. Ideal conditions for them outdoors should be warm and humid with high rainfall. They may be used as houseplants also, but attention should be paid to humidity in the air.

Right: Geonoma interrupta, *in habitat, Choapan, Oaxaca, Mexico.*

Geonoma orbignyana

Features

Growing at incredibly high elevations, up to 10,000 feet (3,000m), in the Andes Mountains of Central and South America this often stunted palm could never be described as beautiful. It has a slim trunk, a few inches in diameter, and a much reduced crown with just a few stiff, pinnate leaves with pointed leaflets. The stunted nature of this palm is a result of the high altitude and the consequent exposure to cold and harsh conditions. The inflorescence is very large for the size of the palm and carries round fruits, black when ripe, less than ½ inch (1cm) in diameter.

Cultivation

The round seeds should germinate in a few weeks if mixed with moist peat and kept in the dark. Fresh seeds are best. Young plants grow slowly and are not easy to maintain in good condition, perhaps because of some particular unknown requirement. It is, after all, a very specialized habitat.

Right: Geonoma orbignyana, *in habitat, at 7,870 feet (2,400m), Zamorra to Loja road, Ecuador.*

Geonoma undata

Red crownshaft palm

Features

This delightful palm has been much written about since it was first seen along the famous "Inca Trail" in Ecuador, where curiously there is a prevalence of red-hued shrubs, grasses, and other plants. Here it grows in a tiny pocket of vegetation at high altitude, surrounded by encroaching farmland; it can only be a matter of time

before the entire area is engulfed. It is also seen elsewhere and is not uncommon in many mountainous areas of Central and South America. Brown, beige, and green crownshaft versions are also encountered in different areas along its range. It grows to around 30 feet (10m) tall and the solitary trunk is only 4 inches (10cm) in diameter, surmounted in the most choice specimens by a crownshaft of cherry red. The fruits are ½ inch (1cm) long, oval, and black when ripe.

Cultivation

Easy to germinate and difficult to maintain, it is definitely one for the enthusiast.

Right: Geonoma undata, *in habitat, "Inca Trail," Villacabamba, Ecuador.*

Geonoma
weberbaueri

Features

A mountain palm from the Andes in the top half of
South America. It is a somewhat variable and
untidy palm, with leathery, pinnate leaves that have
leaflets of different widths, reduced and sometimes
stunted by the tough conditions of its habitat. It grows to about 30 feet (10m) tall,
with a solitary trunk up to 4 inches (10cm) in diameter. Its main claim to fame is that
it grows at an altitude of up to 10,500 feet (3,200m), one of the highest for any
palm. Here it can be seen emerging from other stunted vegetation and suffering
high winds and intense cold. The fruits are carried on comparatively large inflorescences and are about ½ inch (1cm) in diameter, round, and black when ripe.

Cultivation

The easy part is germinating the seeds. However, perhaps due to its unique habitat,
it seems to require particular conditions not easily supplied in cultivation. For this

reason plants seem to malinger after a
promising start and generally go into
decline.

Above: Geonoma weberbaueri, *in habitat, Santa
    Barbara, Ecuador.*
Left: The fruits are black when ripe.

Guihaia argyrata

Features

An attractive and unusual small palm from southern China, described as recently as 1982. It has a small trunk, sometimes underground, and a crown of tidy, circular, fan-shaped leaves, the leaflets being roof- instead of valley-shaped, almost unique in palmate palms. The upper surface is dark green, the underside bright silvery-white, or sometimes pale brown. The small fruits are carried among the leaves and are black when ripe. It grows on limestone hills and cliffs around Guilin, an area popular with tourists, somehow finding a purchase in tiny ledges and crevices.

Cultivation

A specialized habitat such as this would seem to require equally special conditions in cultivation. The seeds germinate erratically and the subsequent growth of the plants is the same; a row of them will all grow at different rates. Plants grow brilliantly at Fairchild Tropical Garden in Florida, perhaps the coral soil mimics the limestone of home.

Above: Guihaia argyrata, *Fairchild Tropical Garden, Florida, USA.*

Left: The leaf underside is silvery white. In habitat, Guilin, China.

Hedescepe canterburyana
Umbrella palm

Features

Sharing the tiny Lord Howe Island off the east coast of Australia with the considerably more famous Kentia palms, this attractive species has a distinctly ringed trunk, up to about 13 feet (4m) tall, a swollen crownshaft, and a stiff crown of erect leaves with upward pointing leaflets, presenting a wonderful sight as it clings to the steep hillsides and mountain tops of its native home. Very slow growing, it is alas not much seen in cultivation. The fruits, borne on inflorescences that appear below the crownshaft, are dark red when ripe, 1½ inches (4cm) long, and oval in shape.

Cultivation

The seeds, which are oval and about 1 inch (3cm) in length, take a long time to ripen and are erratic to germinate, sometimes taking many months. Seedlings grow quite well, however, and it is worth the wait. Good as houseplants and excellent in the subtropical garden, they should be more widely grown.

Right: Hedescepe canterburyana, *cultivated, garden of Mrs. Pauleen Sullivan, Ventura, CA, USA.*

Howea belmoreana

Sentry palm

Features

Considerably less well-known than its cousin the Kentia palm, it shares the same attributes in terms of care. From Lord Howe Island 500 miles off the east coast of Australia, the Sentry palm has a slim, solitary, dark green, prominently ringed trunk, and grows up to about 30 feet (10m) in height. There is no crownshaft. The leathery, pinnate leaves bear upright leaflets which form a v-shape along the rachis and are quite distinctive. The fruits which are carried on a pendulous, simple unbranched inflorescence are oval, about 1½ inches (4cm) in length, and red-brown when ripe.

Cultivation

The fruits take a long time, perhaps a few years, to ripen. They germinate erratically, sometimes taking weeks, sometimes months to sprout. Seedlings grow slowly but steadily and they are easy to care for. As interior plants they are unsurpassed, tolerating low light and general neglect; they also make wonderful garden subjects in subtropical to warm-temperate climates.

Above: Howea belmoreana, *cultivated, California, USA.*

Right: The beautiful Lord Howe Island.

Howea forsteriana
Kentia palm

Features

Popular and familiar as an interior palm for 100 years, it can be seen, usually planted two or three plants to the pot, in offices and homes across the world. In habitat on Lord Howe Island, it grows to a tall tree, up to 50 feet (15m) in height, with a slim, solitary trunk, and noticeable white rings, the scars of fallen leaves. The big, leathery, feather-shaped leaves have leaflets that are held flat or drooping and are dark green. The 2 inch (5cm) long oval fruits are produced on pendulous, simple flower stalks and may be on the tree for some years before they ripen, when they are reddish-brown.

Cultivation

Perhaps the most commonly seen palm in interior decoration, it withstands drought, low light, and general neglect. It grows slowly taking many years to outgrow its space. The seeds are slow and erratic to germinate and much patience is required.

Above: Howea forsteriana, in habitat, Lord Howe Island.
Right: Collecting Howea seeds.
Far right: Kentia palm ready for sale.

Hyophorbe indica

Features

One of a small genus of five species, all from the Mascarene Islands off the east African coast, that are popular in cultivation because of their often bizarre trunk shapes. *H. indica* is from Reunion Island where it grows at low altitude. The trunk, up to about 15 feet (5m) in height, is slim, smooth, and pale brown, with a noticeable crownshaft. The small crown consists of just a few leaves, leathery in texture and dark green. The inflorescence is produced below the crownshaft and carries fragrant, creamy white flowers followed by fruits, beaked at one end, about 1 inch (3cm) long, and orange to brown when ripe.

Cultivation

The oval seeds germinate readily and easily and the seedlings grow rather fast. They make good and interesting house plants; outdoors they prefer a tropical climate tolerating drought but benefiting from an adequate supply of water.

Right: Hyophorbe indica, *cultivated, Jardin Botanico Robert y Catherine Wilson, Puntarenas, Costa Rica.*

Hyophorbe lagenicaulis
Bottle palm

Features

Famous for its strange, swollen, bottle-shaped trunk, this fascinating palm is widely cultivated across the tropics and is often seen in botanic gardens as well as in private collections. It grows to about 10 feet (3m) or more in height, and the ringed, pale brown trunk is enlarged and bottle shaped. The leaves with their dark green leathery leaflets twist in a characteristic fashion. There is a prominent crownshaft

beneath which the inflorescences appear producing white flowers followed by oval fruits, which are carmine red when ripe. It is almost extinct in its home on Round Island and its only chance of survival is in cultivation.

Cultivation

The oval seeds germinate easily and quickly if fresh and seedling growth is steady. The unusual shape is apparent from a very early age. Useful as houseplants or conservatory plants when small, outdoors they require full sun, a tropical climate, and while they can withstand drought conditions prefer permanent access to ground water.

Left: Hyophorbe lagenicaulis, *cultivated, Singapore.*

Hyophorbe verschaffeltii
Spindle palm

Features

Similar in some respects to the Bottle palm, the trunk is much slimmer, spindle-shaped and ringed, with a glaucous green, slightly swollen crownshaft. It grows taller than its cousin, to at least 20 feet (6m), and the leaves are fuller and more abundant. On its native Rodriguez Island it is now, sadly, all but extinct, though happily it is widely cultivated throughout the tropics. The flower stalk grows just below the crownshaft and produces scented orange flowers followed by oval fruits, an inch (3cm) or so long, and bright red when ripe.

Cultivation

The beaked spindle-shaped seeds germinate easily if fresh. The young plants grow quickly and reliably and are sometimes sold several to a pot as houseplants. As such, they are tolerant and undemanding. As exterior plants they require a sunny position in the tropical or subtropical garden.

Above: Hyophorbe
verschaffeltii, *John DeMott
Garden, Homestead,
Florida, USA.*
*Right and far right: The
swollen crownshaft.*

A Pocket Guide to Palms

Hyphaene thebaica
Doum or Gingerbread palm

Features

Unmistakable palms of the savanna of north and east Africa, their unique characteristic is their branching habit, resulting in a plant as wide as it is tall, often with countless crowns of strongly recurved, blue-green costapalmate leaves. The leaf stalks are thorny, the fruits are quite large, up to 4 inches (10cm) long, and pear-shaped, orange when ripe, with a smell reminiscent of gingerbread. A mature tree is a splendid sight indeed set against the blue sky of the desert.

Cultivation

The seeds should be removed from the fibrous fruit and soaked for several days before planting. Germination is erratic and may be quite fast. A long sinker is produced enabling the fledgling plant to find underground water, so choose a deep pot or, better yet, plant into its permanent position in the ground. Very slow growing.

Above: Hyphaene thebaica, *semi-cultivated, Atbara, Sudan, with the author.*
Right: The pear-shaped fruits are red-brown when ripe.

Palms

Iriartea deltoidea

Features

A beautiful palm commonly seen growing on the steep and wet mountains all over the western half of upper South America and Central America. The trunk is solitary and to about 80 feet (25m) tall and about a foot (25 or 30 cm) in diameter, sometimes swollen in the middle. It can be pale brown to white and often has stilt roots to support it. The superb leaves are densely plumose in appearance like giant bottle

brushes. The distinctive inflorescence appears below the leaves and is the shape of a horn. The flowers are followed by fruits some ½ to 1 inch (2 to 3cm) in diameter, round, and greenish yellow when ripe.

Cultivation

The round seeds should be sown fresh and they will germinate within a few weeks. Seedling growth is quite slow but speeds up as the plant gets bigger. An interesting pot plant for the humid greenhouse but, it seems, rather difficult as an outdoor subject except in areas climactically close to its original home.

Left: Iriartea deltoidea, *in habitat, Quevedo, Ecuador. Note the horn-shaped bracts.*

Johannesteijsmannia altifrons
"Joey"

Features

A beautiful, simple-leaved palm from the Malaysian rainforest that is much sought after for use in tropical landscaping. The big diamond- or paddle-shaped leaves are strongly pleated and arise straight from the ground with no appreciable trunk. These can be up to 13 feet (4m) or more long by 6 feet (2m) wide, and have green undersides. The fruits grow on inflorescences among the leaves, are round and warty in appearance, about 1½ inches (4cm) in diameter, and brown when ripe. These arresting understory palms seem to prefer ridge tops and slopes and in some areas are locally common.

Cultivation

The round seeds are becoming more widely available as interest grows in these stunning plants. If planted in moist peat, kept warm and damp, they should sprout within a

few weeks. Seedling growth is quite fast and the characteristic leaf shape is soon evident. It makes a good houseplant kept in a humid conservatory and is surprisingly hardy to cool conditions.

Left: Johannesteijsmannia altifrons, *cultivated, Singapore Botanic Gardens.*

Johannesteijsmannia perakensis
Trunked Joey

Features

Similar in most respects to *Johannesteijsmannia altifrons* with roughly diamond-shaped leaves, this native of Perak Province in northwest Malaysia has a slim trunk to about 10 feet (3m) or so tall. It is usually found on wet slopes or hillsides in light forest, a clue to its cultivation requirements. The fruits, which are corky or warty and brown when ripe, are about 2 inches (5cm) in diameter, each containing one round seed, which is smooth and pale brown. One local use is that of a temporary umbrella, but the large leaves are also used as thatching for native huts. In some areas it is quite common.

Cultivation

The round seeds if planted fresh will germinate within a few weeks. The young plants should be potted up into a peaty mix and moved to a brighter spot, though out of direct sunlight. They can be used as houseplants for a time, though a shady position in the tropical and moist garden would suit them ideally.

Right: Johannesteijsmannia perakensis, *cultivated, Singapore Botanic Gardens.*

A Pocket Guide to Palms

Juania australis
Chonta palm

Features
Interesting palm if for no other reason than the fact that it grows only on one tiny island, Juan Fernandez (sometimes called Robinson Crusoe's Island), off the coast of Chile. There it grows on steep cliffs, on ridges and in gullies, safe from predation

by either man or goat. It is virtually unknown in cultivation but, in the wild at least, it has a rather windswept look. The trunk is noticeably ringed with old leaf scars, and the feather-shaped leaves seem to be permanently battered by wind, however, in cultivation it presents a more rested appearance. The inflorescences appear among the leaves and carry round fruits ⅔ inch (1.5cm) in diameter, orange-red when ripe.

Cultivation
Seeds, which are in very short supply, germinate erratically sometimes taking months to sprout, and subsequent seedling growth is slow, though does speed up as the plant matures. Definitely one for the enthusiast.

Left: Juania australis, *cultivated, Chile.*

Jubaea chilensis
Chilean wine palm

Features

When Charles Darwin first encountered this hardy palm on his voyage on board *The Beagle*, he saw hundreds of thousands of them covering every available hillside. Populations are now much reduced, but stable, and still very impressive. It is a massive palm, up to 50 feet (15m) tall, and with a trunk up to 3 feet (1m) in diameter, narrowing after reaching maturity, but huge by any standards. The smooth trunk has obscure diamond-shaped leaf scars and is surmounted by a large crown of glossy, feather-shaped leaves. The inflorescences arise among the leaves and produce countless thousands of round fruits, 1½ inches (4cm) in diameter, which are yellow when ripe.

Cultivation

The round seeds, ¾ inch (2cm) in diameter, are exported as edible nuts to the supermarkets of Europe and the USA. They germinate quite easily and growth is steady, though it can be 20–25 years before a trunk is produced. It is probably the most cold-hardy feather palm.

Above: Jubaea chilensis, *in habitat, Chile.*
Right: In some areas Jubaea *is extremely common.*

Jubaeopsis caffra
Pondoland palm

Features

An unusual palm, found growing at only a few almost inaccessible sites in
Pondoland in South Africa, usually overhanging river banks. It is a clustering
species, to about 20 feet (6m) tall, with a number of slim trunks bearing feather-
shaped leaves. The flowers grow among the leaves and these are followed by
round fruits resembling those of *Jubaea* to which it is closely related, about 1 inch
(3cm) in diameter, brown when ripe and containing an oily flesh. Expeditions to col-
lect the seed have to cope with, among other things, swollen rivers, mosquitoes
and crocodiles, hence they are somewhat uncommon in cultivation.

Cultivation

Not only are the seeds
hard to come by, they are
also difficult to germinate,
sometimes taking many
weeks. Seedling growth
is slow but steady and
the palm is grown mainly
as a curiosity by
collectors.

Right: Jubaeopsis caffra, *cultivated,
Tzaneen, Northern Province,
South Africa.*

Kentiopsis oliviformis

Features

A tall, up to 100 feet (30m), slim, solitary, elegant palm from central New Caledonia where it grows in small restricted rocky areas. It is mainly a collector's palm though it has great potential for more general decorative use. The trunk is noticeably ringed and tapers upward from an enlarged base, the leaves are feather-shaped and upright, above a noticeable crownshaft. The large inflorescence appears among the leaves and carries fragrant white flowers followed by fruits the size and shape of small olives, bright red when fully ripe.

The name comes from its general resemblance to the Kentia palm.

Cultivation

The oval seeds are slow to germinate and require conditions of warmth and moisture. Once sprouted the seedlings grow slowly. Suitable for the tropical garden this palm is grown mainly by enthusiasts, but is beginning to appear more generally. It is a good looking species and deserves to be more widely known.

Right: Kentiopsis oliviformis, *cultivated, Florida, USA.*

Kerriodoxa elegans
White elephant palm

Features

This beautiful palm is restricted to a small area on the tourist island of Phuket in Thailand where it grows in the Waterfall Gardens, and a further area on the adjacent mainland. One cannot fail to be impressed by the large 6 feet (2m) diameter circular spreading leaves held flat, supported on black petioles, dull green above, but bright silvery white beneath. In fact it grows to 20 feet (6m) in height but looks best before

it grows a trunk when the leaves can be seen to advantage. The round fruits are about 2 inches (5cm) in diameter, orange when ripe, and with a rough surface.

Cultivation

The round seeds germinate quite quickly if fresh and subsequent seedling growth is steady. The first leaves are already quite wide and soon show the characteristic silvery underside. Definitely one for the shady, tropical garden or quite splendid in the humid conservatory.

Left: Kerriodoxa elegans, *cultivated, Fairchild Tropical Garden, Florida, USA, with Emma Gibbons for scale.*

Laccospadix australasica

Atherton palm

Features

Sure to become more popular as it is more widely available, this pretty, small, solitary, or suckering palm has a slim trunk just an inch or so in diameter and an attractive crown of upright, stiff, feathery leaves. It comes from the rainforests of northeast Queensland in Australia where it is locally common but alas is not often seen outside its native country. The flower stalks are simple, undivided and strongly arching, bending down under the weight of the oval fruits, which are bright cherry-red when ripe. The plant grows to about 25 feet (7 or 8m) in height and is extremely ornamental.

Cultivation

The oval seeds must be sown fresh as they lose their viability very quickly. Under these conditions they germinate in a few weeks, though the young plants grow slowly. Suitable as houseplants, they tolerate low light conditions well; outside they prefer warm moist conditions and do best in shade. Cool tolerant.

Right: Laccospadix australasica, *cultivated, Durban Botanic Garden.*

Latania loddigesii
Blue Latan palm

Features

This small genus contains just three species, all from the tropical Mascarene Islands where they are now highly endangered due to indiscriminate cutting. The Blue Latan palm from Round Island is a handsome tree, to about 40 feet (12m) in height with a slim trunk, ringed, surmounted by a crown of large, blue-green, stiff, fan-shaped leaves, the petioles of which are covered with pale fluffy tomentum. The fruits,

which are produced in clusters among the leaves, are the size and shape of plums, dark brown when ripe. The attractive seeds within look carved and sculpted.

Cultivation

These palms are easy to grow. The seeds sprout readily in a few weeks, and the seedlings also grow rather fast. The young leaves are stiff and dark green, edged with red. Suitable for the tropical garden, or the conservatory in cooler climates.

Left: Latania loddigesii, *cultivated, Fairchild Tropical Garden, Florida, USA.*

Latania lontaroides
Red latan palm

Features
The red of the name is especially apparent in the young plants, the leaves of which are highly attractive. From Reunion Island where it is almost extinct, it is fortunately quite widely grown in cultivation and is frequently seen in botanic gardens. The adult leaves are blue-green and stiffly held, the trunk, to about 40 feet (12m) in height, is slim and noticeably ringed with old leaf scars. The inflorescences appear among the leaves and carry large, oval, plum-like fruits, each containing two or three almond-shaped seeds, which have a sculpted appearance.

Cultivation
If planted fresh, the seeds germinate quickly and easily when mixed with moist peat and kept warm. Once sprouted, the young plants require bright conditions and an adequate supply of water. Just wonderful in the tropical garden, they also make useful and pretty house or conservatory plants.

Above and right: Latania lontaroides, *cultivated, National Tropical Botanical Garden, Kalaheo, Kauai, Hawaii.*

Latania verschaffeltii
Yellow latan palm

Features

The intense yellow of the plants is apparent from a very early age. As the tree matures, however, it is lost and the stiff, fan-shaped leaves are green or slightly blue-green, with the petioles and leaf bases covered with pale, woolly tomentum. The slim trunk, which grows to about 35 feet (10 or 12m) in height, is clearly ringed with the scars of fallen leaves. The plum-like fruits are borne on inflorescences that arise among the leaves, containing two or three seeds, which like the others in the genus, appear sculpted as though carved with a knife. This handsome palm comes from Rodriguez Island where it is now extremely rare.

Cultivation

Like those of the others in the genus the seeds should be planted as fresh as possible and they will germinate within a few weeks. The young plants are an attractive yellow and make interesting plants for the home or conservatory. In the tropical garden they require full sun.

Left: Latania verschaffeltii, *cultivated, National Tropical Botanical Garden, Kalaheo, Kauai, Hawaii.*

Licuala grandis
Ruffled fan palm

Features

Licuala is a large genus of a hundred or more species, occurring widely across south and east Asia where they grow as understory plants in rainforests. Popular as a beautiful houseplant, *L. grandis* has a slim trunk to 15 feet tall and a crown of wonderful, almost circular, undivided, pleated, grass-green leaves, up to 24 inches (60cm) in diameter. The edge of the leaf is notched, and the small round fruits, bright red when ripe, hang down from among the leaf bases. It occurs naturally in the Solomon Islands where it grows in large colonies.

Cultivation

Widely available now as an attractive houseplant, it is also easily grown from seed, which if fresh germinates within a few weeks in moist conditions. The young plants grow slowly to begin with but speed up as they get larger. The leaves are strap-shaped to begin with and gain their characteristic shape with age. Requires humidity to prevent the leaf tips from browning, and tropical conditions if grown in a garden.

Above: Licuala grandis, *cultivated, Fairchild Tropical Garden, Florida, USA.*
Right: The ripe fruits are bright red.

A Pocket Guide to Palms

Licuala orbicularis

Features

From the moist rainforest in Borneo the flat and circular, highly glossy leaves of this sought-after species are breathtaking when seen for the first time in the forest gloom. It does not form a trunk and the few leaves grow directly from an underground rootstock; they can be up to 3 feet (1m) in diameter. One unfortunate local use is that of a temporary umbrella. It is heartbreaking to see the leaves discarded on the jungle floor after a brief downpour. The small round fruits are about ½ inch (1cm) in diameter and grow on flower stalks from among the leaves. They are bright cherry-red when ripe.

Cultivation

Very much a collector's item and not the easiest palm to grow, the small round seeds germinate in a few weeks or months, but must be fresh to succeed. The young plants grow extremely slowly and it is a long time before they have the char-

acteristic shape of the adult leaf. In the tropical garden they require low light and very moist, wind-free conditions.

Left: Licuala orbicularis, *in habitat, Kuching, Borneo, with Tim Hatch.*

Licuala peltata

Features

From India, Thailand, and Malaysia, this is another entire-leaved species though there is also a split-leaf form. The trunk is slim, and both solitary and clustering forms are known. The circular leaves can be up to 5 feet (1.5m) in diameter, strongly pleated, and held on strong petioles with sharp spines along the edges. The leading edge of the leaf is toothed. The long arching inflorescences extend well beyond the leaves and produce large quantities of small round fruits, bright red when ripe, about ½ inch (1cm) in diameter.

Cultivation

The round seeds, planted fresh, germinate in a couple of months, and the young seedlings grow reasonably slowly. Very much a palm for the tropics or subtropics it would be wonderful in a sheltered spot, in shade to begin with, and out of the wind which could damage its large leaves. Also an attractive palm for the humid conservatory.

Right: Licuala peltata, *cultivated, Fairchild Tropical Garden, Florida, USA.*

A Pocket Guide to Palms

Licuala spinosa

Features

Much easier to grow than many others in the genus it is not as pretty but still an interesting palm for the tropical garden, also useful as a houseplant. The leaves are split deeply to the base into about ten or twelve segments, with square and notched tips. They grow on clustering slim trunks, to about 12 feet (3 or 4m) in height. The leaf stalks are thorny and should be handled with care. The overall effect is one of a dense, rounded bush of attractive foliage further improved by bright red fruits on long arching inflorescences, which extend way beyond the leaves.

Cultivation

The small round fruits each contain a single seed. These need to be sown as fresh as possible; stale seeds may not sprout for a long time, or at all. The young plants seem quite tough and grow slowly but steadily, finally gaining the characteristic shape of the adult leaves. It is a good houseplant, tolerating low light and neglect. Humidity will avoid browning of the leaflet tips.

Left: Licuala spinosa, *cultivated, Fairchild Tropical Garden, Florida, USA.*

Livistona australis
Australian fan palm

Features

One of a genus of some thirty species occurring widely across southeast Asia and Australia with one in northeast Africa. *L. australis* is from the east of Australia where it grows in large colonies in rainforests, often in swampy ground. Growing to 65 feet (20m) or more in height, the slim trunk is covered with old leaf bases at the top, smooth below. The fan-shaped leaves, supported on thorny petioles are 3 feet (1m) or so in diameter, and the fruits, red-brown when ripe and ½ inch (1cm) in diameter, hang down from among the leaves in large bunches.

Cultivation

Easily grown from fresh seed, it makes a good houseplant though the petiole thorns may be seen as a detriment to use in the home. It grows in warm-temperate to tropical climates and will tolerate light frosts. Popular across the globe.

Above: Livistona australis, cultivated, Giardino Hanbury, La Mortola, Liguria, Italy.
Right: A juvenile plant, in South Africa.

Livistona chinensis

Chinese fan palm

Features

Well known for a hundred and fifty years, this attractive fan palm was popular with the Victorians who first recognized its qualities as an indoor plant and used it to great effect in the salons of the Palm Court orchestra. It is a stout tree to 20 feet (6m) tall, has a ringed trunk marked with the scars of fallen leaves, and a large crown of fan-shaped leaves with drooping leaflet tips, giving rise to its other name of Fountain palm. The leaf stalks are thorny and the large clusters of round fruits are ½ to ¾ inch (1 to 2cm) in diameter, lead blue when ripe, and hang down from among the leaves.

Cultivation

An easy and rewarding houseplant that is tolerant of low light and neglect. It is easily grown from seed, which should be planted fresh. The young plants grow quickly, the first leaves are strap-shaped and it can be a while before the first fan leaves appear. Outside, it is suitable for warm-temperate to tropical climates.

Above: Livistona chinensis *fruits.*

Left: Livistona chinensis, *cultivated, Florida, USA.*

Livistona decipiens
Ribbon fan palm

Features

This species, from Australia, has fan-shaped leaves, which are a fresh green, with strongly drooping tips, making it unmistakable when seen from a distance. As a young plant it can be recognized by the strongly costapalmate leaves which give it an unusual look. The trunk grows up to 65 feet (20m) or so tall, 16 inches (40cm) in diameter, and is covered with scars of old leaves. The inflorescences arise from among the leaves and produce generous quantities of round fruits ½ inch (1cm) in diameter, blue-black when ripe, and each containing a single seed.

Cultivation

The small round seeds germinate easily and quickly, subsequent seedling growth is also fast. Though having a slightly untidy look it makes an excellent houseplant and needs the minimum of care and attention. It is an arresting subject in the garden where it does best in tropical to warm-temperate conditions.

Right: Livistona decipiens, *cultivated, Caracas Botanic Garden, Venezuela.*

Livistona jenkinsiana
Jenkins fan palm

Features

A little known but recently rediscovered, handsome fan palm from northern India where it grows, often at some altitude, in forest in the foothills of the Himalayas. It also occurs in northern Thailand and much of Southeast Asia. In wind free locations the undamaged fan leaves present a pretty sight, well over 6 feet (2m) in diameter, with many segments. Usually however, and once above the surrounding vegetation, the trees present a less attractive appearance with the crowns wind-blown and damaged. The petioles are thorny, and the fruits appear from among the leaves, hanging down in clusters. They are round, ¾ to 1 inch (2 to 3cm) in diameter, and leaden blue when ripe.

Cultivation

The round seeds, about ⅔ inch (1.5cm) in diameter, germinate rather easily if sown fresh and the seedlings grow fast also. This species is new to cultivation but should make a good addition to the range of cultivated *Livistona*.

Above: The lead blue fruits.

Left: Livistona jenkinsiana, *semi-cultivated, Kalimpong, W. Bengal, India.*

Livistona mariae (incl. L. rigida)
Central Australian cabbage palm

Features

From a few locations in the deserts of central and northern Australia comes this relict species, surviving where there is permanent underground water. They grow to about 80 feet (25m) in height, with a small crown of ragged fan-shaped leaves. One interesting characteristic is that the leaves of young plants are deep red. This is lost as the plants mature as the adult leaves revert to green. The conditions in their native habitat are intensely hot and dry, an indication of their requirements in cultivation.

Cultivation

It is a good idea to soak the seeds of all desert palms prior to planting, simulating the rainfall that often triggers germination. Once sprouted the seedlings grow slowly, but, in the bright light they require, soon turn an attractive shade of red. More and more widely seen now in botanic gardens around the world.

Left: In full sun the young plants of Livistona mariae *are quite red.*

Livistona rotundifolia
Footstool palm

Features

A distinctive species with smaller, fan-shaped leaves carried in a long, deep crown, it is native to Malaysia and Indonesia where it grows in rain-forests, often appearing above surrounding vegetation. The trunk is slim and noticeably ringed with old leaf scars, the petioles are thorny and the ¾ inch (2cm) diameter round fruits hang down plentifully on long strings from among the leaves. They are bright red when ripe, and add to the attractiveness of this elegant palm.

Cultivation

Planted fresh in moist peat, the small round seeds germinate in a few weeks. Seedlings grow at a satisfactory rate and soon attain the "footstool" look of the common name. They make great houseplants, easy to care for, and slow growing. Outside they require tropical or subtropical conditions.

Above: Livistona rotundifolia, cultivated, Bagdograh, W. Bengal, India.
Right: The ripe fruits are bright red.

Lodoicea maldivica
Double coconut

Features

The Valley de Mai on Praslin where these remarkable palms grow is now firmly established on the tourist circuit for visitors to the Seychelle Islands. They present a truly remarkable sight and sound as the huge fan leaves crash about in the wind. The seeds are the largest in the vegetable kingdom weighing up to 44 lb (20kg) and may stay several years on the parent tree before they are ripe. The trees themselves have tall trunks, up to about 80 feet (25m), which are rather thick. Male and female flowers are on separate plants and local legend has it that they go in search of one another on moonlit nights.

Cultivation

These large palms grow unreasonably slowly and are grown mainly by botanic gardens or committed enthusiasts. The huge seeds are half buried in moist peat and with luck, produce the first thick root after several months. Subsequent growth is very slow and it could take 20 years before a trunk begins to form.

Above: A young Lodoicea maldivica *in Singapore Botanic Gardens.*

Right: The seed of this palm is the largest in the vegetable kingdom.

Lytocaryum weddellianum

Miniature coconut palm

Features

Truly delightful small palms from one tiny area of Brazil where they are under extreme threat as their habitat is encroached on by farming. They have a slim trunk just an inch or so thick and up to 16 feet (5m) in height. The crown is composed of the most delicate looking feather-shaped leaves with narrow leaflets, glossy green above and silvery beneath. They are held upright, though the older leaves may droop. The spathe arises from among the leaves and after flowering produces fruits like tiny coconuts the weight of which causes the fruiting branch to hang down.

Cultivation

The small seeds, like coconuts, have three pores at one end and it is from one of these that the first leaves will appear, after several weeks in moist and warm conditions. These palms are rather slow growing but well worth the wait. They make good houseplants and will grow outdoors in climates from cool-temperate to tropical.

Above and Left: Lytocaryum weddellianum, *Jacques Deleuze Garden, Corsica, France.*

Mauritia flexuosa
Morete palm

Features

A totally amazing palm, widespread and locally
common in the top half of South America. It
has a stout trunk and the leaves look somewhat like exploding fireworks, because they are
strongly costapalmate, which sends the leaf
segments off in all directions. The tree grows to
about 80 feet (25m) tall, the trunk is smooth
with obscure rings, and there are usually a few dead leaves hanging down from the
crown. The fruits are oval, about 2½ inches (6cm) long, orange-brown when ripe,
and covered with tiny overlapping scales. The fleshy layer beneath this soon rots
away exposing the round seed within.

Cultivation

Fresh seeds germinate easily and quickly, the seedlings grow rather fast. Essentially

a palm for the humid tropics, it
would certainly do best in areas
of high rainfall. It can be grown in
the conservatory for a few years.

*Above: Mauritia flexuosa in habitat, near
Gualaquiza, Ecuador.*
*Left: The beautiful fruits are covered with
overlapping scales.*

Mauritiella armata

Features

An attractive, easily recognized, clustering species, one of three in the genus, like a small multi-trunked version of the Morete palm, often seen growing in swampy ground or in flooded areas of the Amazon region of South America. Reaching them can present quite a challenge and usually involves getting wet. The slim trunks are to about 65 feet (20m) tall and perhaps 4 inches (10cm) in diameter, covered, at least in the lower part, with root spines. The leaves are costapalmate with the leaf

segments radiating outward in all directions. The round fruits, which are produced from below the leaves, are covered with small overlapping scales. They are carmine red when fully ripe and about 1 inch (3cm) in diameter.

Cultivation

Not widely known in cultivation, this attractive palm would do well in a humid climate with high rainfall. The fresh seeds germinate readily in a moist, peaty substrate and the seedlings grow at a reasonable speed.

Left: Mauritiella armata, *in habitat, Baeza-Lago Agrio road, Ecuador.*

Medemia argun
Nubian desert palm

Features

This palm from the arid deserts of Sudan was long believed extinct until a special expedition was mounted to look for it. The search was successful and several thousand trees were found along with countless seeds, which were distributed around the world, contributing to the species' survival. It is a handsome palm, tall and solitary, with a crown of blue-green costapalmate leaves, reminiscent of *Hyphaene* and *Bismarckia* to which it is closely related. The seeds are the size and shape of plums, dark purple to black when ripe, and pierced through with red on the inside. The petioles are bright yellow and the trunk is bare.

Cultivation

The large oval seeds germinate very quickly and put down a long sinker. The seedlings, which grow steadily, require very warm to hot conditions, and the bare minimum of water. They are probably best planted in their permanent position as soon as possible.

Above: Medemia argun *in habitat, Nubian Desert, Sudan, with the author.*
Above left: The fruits are produced in large quantities.
Left: The plum-sized fruits look to have been run through with a rusty needle.

A Pocket Guide to Palms

Metroxylon sagu
Sago palm

Features
Originating in the Philippines but now so widely cultivated in the tropics that its precise origins are obscure, this economically useful, clustering species produces good quality sago from the split trunk, harvested just as the tree is about to flower. If left to grow and not cut down this palm produces attractive, round, scale-covered fruits about 2 inches (5cm) in diameter. The trunk dies after fruiting to be replaced by others in the group. The leaves are upright and feather-shaped, the trunks are about 25 feet (8m) in height and they grow naturally in swampy conditions. They are fast growing trees providing a continual supply of nutritious food for many villagers in the wet tropics.

Cultivation
The large seeds should be planted when fresh, and the young plants grow very quickly. They require hot, humid, and swampy conditions to succeed and are probably best suited to the botanic garden.

Right: Metroxylon sagu, *cultivated, Singapore Botanic Garden.*

Nannorrhops
ritchiana

Mazari palm

Features

A curious palm from the deserts and hills of Pakistan, Afghanistan, and some other Middle Eastern countries. It used to be much more common than it is now, but continual cutting of the leaves for fibers has decimated the populations. The leaves are a waxy blue-green in color and, in the wild at least, plants are usually short and stunted, often covering huge areas. In cultivation they can grow much larger, reaching a few meters in height. It is a suckering species, branching after flowering. The fruits are a centimeter or two in diameter, red-brown when ripe. Some time ago, three species were "lumped" into one. This may prove to have been a mistake as there are clearly at least two "forms."

Cultivation

The round pea-sized seeds germinate quite easily after a good soak in water. However, the seedlings are erratic in their growth habit. Some are fast, others really slow and stunted. They seem to shock easily and die for no apparent reason. They resent root disturbance. One of the world's most cold-hardy palms.

Above: Nannorrhops ritchiana, *in habitat, Pakistan.*

Right: Camel, laden with cut leaves of Nannorrhops.

A Pocket Guide to Palms

Normanbya normanbyi
Black palm

Features

A northeastern Australian palm with a solitary trunk and a handsome crown of plumose leaves above a prominent crownshaft. It grows to about 65 feet (20m) in height and prefers swampy areas with a high rainfall. Formerly used by aborigines for the durable, black timber of the trunk which was used for building and the making of weapons, it is seen increasingly often in botanic gardens and private collections. The inflorescence is produced from below the leaves and after flowering carries clusters of oval fruits, which are pinkish-purple when ripe.

Cultivation

Not the easiest palm to grow, the oval seeds germinate erratically and may take several months to sprout. They require warmth and humidity. The seedlings grow quite speedily however. Grows best in a humid tropical environment in tropics or subtropics in areas of high rainfall and is said to benefit from regular applications of fertilizer.

Left: Normanbya normanbyi, *cultivated, Singapore Botanic Garden.*

Nypa fruticans
Nypa palm

Features

A curious estuarine palm, it grows in brackish water where river meets sea in India, Sri Lanka, and Australia, and is semi-cultivated across the tropics. It has a subterranean trunk usually submerged in the mud, the leaves appearing to grow straight from the ground. Locally, economically important, all parts of the plant are used for one purpose or another. The petioles are very thick, strong, and round, supporting 25 feet (7 or 8m) long, feather-shaped leaves help upright. The flowering structure is extraordinary; the spherical, football sized fruiting head has large individual fruits tightly packed on the surface. The unripe seeds are sweet and edible.

Cultivation

Unusually, the seeds germinate in position on the fruiting head and push themselves

away as they grow. At this time they need to be planted into soft mud, where they will continue to grow quite quickly. This is an oddity mainly suitable for the collector or botanic garden.

Above: Nypa fruticans, *cultivated, Montgomery Botanical Center.*
Left: In muddy habitat, mouth of the Salween River, Moulmein, Burma.

A Pocket Guide to Palms

Oenocarpus bataua
Milpesos palm

Features

Frequently seen all over the top half of South America, this big, attractive, solitary tree grows to about 65 feet (20m) tall and has an upright crown of feather-shaped leaves, which are green above and silvery beneath. It is often to be found in swampy or flooded areas and seems quite happy with the base of the trunk under water. Its most distinctive characteristic is the inflorescence, which resembles the tail of a horse, and several grow at any one time. After flowering these produce oval fruits, reddish brown when ripe, from which an alcoholic drink is made locally.

Cultivation

The oval fruits, the size and shape of very large olives, germinate rapidly and the young plant grows easily, requiring an abundance of water and permanently moist soil. The new leaves are an attractive shade of maroon. Not often seen in botanic gardens but definitely worthy of more frequent use.

Above: Oenocarpus bataua, in habitat, Zamora, Ecuador.

Right: The inflorescences are like horse tails.

Oenocarpus mapora
Don Pedrito's palm

Features

Related to but quite dissimilar to the previous palm, this is a clustering species with several trunks forming an open clump. The stems are slim and only to about 30 feet (10m) tall. The feather leaves are broad, green above and silvery below, the inflorescence is shaped like a horse tail and the fruits, the size and shape of olives, are reddish brown when ripe. It is not uncommon in the northwest of South America where it grows in rain forests at low altitude.

Cultivation

Easily grown from seed this is a palm for the wet tropics where it will be found to be fast growing. Suitable as a houseplant when young, it will do best in humid conditions. Young leaves are an attractive dark red when they open, soon turning green.

Right: Oenocarpus mapora, *in habitat, Tena, Ecuador.*

A Pocket Guide to Palms

Parajubaea cocoides

Coco cumbè or Mountain coconut

Features

Not known in the wild, but frequently seen cultivated or semi-cultivated in its native land of Ecuador, especially in parks and gardens, this tall, up to 50 feet (15m), and elegant palm has been compared to the coconut in appearance. With its slim trunk and broad and shiny pinnate leaves it looks too beautiful to be a temperate palm. The fruits, which ripen at all times of the year, are about 2 or 2½ inches (5 or 6 cm) long, oval, and covered with very tough flesh. They hang down from among the leaves in long strings and are yellow-green when ripe. The ridged seeds within are black and extremely hard.

Cultivation

The flesh must be removed from the seeds, which should then be allowed to dry out for a few weeks. Soaking for a few days should improve germination, which is difficult and sometimes extremely slow. It is rather hardy to cool conditions and may also take some frost.

Above: Parajubaea cocoides, cultivated, Quito, Ecuador.
Left: The fruits are produced year round.

Parajubaea torallyi
Janchicoco

Features
Closely related to the palm on the previous
page, this species comes from Bolivia where
it grows at extremely high altitudes in arid
areas and sandstone valleys, often in great
numbers and extremely difficult of access. It
is rarely seen in cultivation and is a little taller
and more robust than Coco cumbè and the
trunk is rougher in young trees. The glossy
green leaves have silvery undersides and arch attractively. The fruits are somewhat
larger, and the seeds, which have three prominent ridges, are eagerly consumed
by the locals, as they taste like coconut. Two varieties have been reported: *P. torallyi*
var. *torallyi* and *P. torallyi* var. *microcarpa*, with rather smaller seeds.

Cultivation
Different ways have been suggested of germinating the stone-hard seeds, including
soaking, filing, cracking, or blowing pure oxy-
gen over them, however, patience seems to
be the best method. Once germinated the
young plants grow at a satisfying rate and are
soon ready to plant out, in temperate or warm-
temperate climates.

Above: Parajubaea torallyi, *in habitat, Pasopaya, Bolivia.*
Right: Fruit and the edible seed.

A Pocket Guide to Palms

Pelagodoxa henryana

Marquesas palm

Features

From the quintessentially tropical Marquesas Islands in the South Pacific comes this beautiful, simple leaved palm. It is a solitary tree with a trunk up to about 16 feet (5m) tall, but it is the beautiful leaves which attract attention; they can be 6½ feet (2m) long and 3 feet (1m) wide and are undivided, though they may be split by the wind. The upper surface is green, the lower, whitish. The large round fruits are warty in appearance and about 2½ or 3 inches (6 or 8cm) in diameter. Very much a collector's item, they are rarely grown and, in any event, suitable only for the tropics.

Cultivation

The round seeds are said to be quite easy to germinate though may require special treatment such as filing or soaking. Even so, they may take some months to sprout. This is a tropical palm which cannot withstand cold, but may be tried in a humid conservatory.

Above: Pelagodoxa henryana, *cultivated, Caracas Botanic Garden, Venezuela.*
Left: The ripe fruits are corky.

Phoenix acaulis

Features

From Nepal and north India this interesting member of a genus of about 20 species does not grow a trunk or at best only a short and partially underground one, the emergent part being covered with old leaf bases. The leaves are grass-green and pinnate, the leaflets widely spaced and, in common with the rest of the genus, the lower ones on each leaf are reduced to sharp spines. The fruits are red when ripe, about ¾ inch (2cm) long, and contain an edible flesh. They are carried on flower stalks, which appear from among the leaves.

Cultivation

The seeds, which are oval and grooved, are becoming more widely available. They germinate soon after planting, but seedling growth is slow. This is not an especially attractive palm and is mainly of interest to collectors because of its trunkless habit. It is occasionally seen cultivated in botanic gardens.

Right: Phoenix acaulis, *in habitat, Nepal.*

A Pocket Guide to Palms

Phoenix canariensis

Canary Island date palm

Features

Originally from the Canary Islands, where it is now rare, this popular palm is grown by the million for the nursery trade. As an outdoor palm, it develops a stout trunk, up to about 65 feet (20m) tall, with a large crown of grass-green leaves that are pinnate with sharp stiletto-like spines for the lower leaflets. The inedible fruits, which are produced in great quantities, are bright orange when ripe and appear on fruit stalks that grow among the leaves. Each great cluster of fruits appears to be supported by a single leaf. It is an impressive palm tree for the temperate to tropical garden or park and is common as a street tree in countries around the world.

Cultivation

Many an enthusiast's first attempts at germinating palm seeds begin with this species. It is easily grown and germinates readily. Subsequent growth is satisfyingly fast and it is an ideal "beginner's palm."

Above: Phoenix canariensis, *semi-cultivated, Canary Islands.*

Right: The heavy bunches of fruit are supported by the leaves.

Phoenix dactylifera
Date palm

Features

Commonly cultivated in many hot dry countries for the commercially important dates, which provide the staple diet for many native people. The suckering trunk is slim and tall, up to about 80 feet (25m), and the crown consists of coarse, pinnate leaves that are a noticeable glaucous-green. The famous fruits, reddish brown when ripe, are produced in large quantities, especially on trees bred for the purpose. Male and female flowers are on different plants and in plantations one male tree is planted for every twenty females.

Cultivation

The seeds from dates, a fruit traditionally eaten at Christmas, can be grown quite easily into attractive houseplants after mixing with moist peat, kept warm and humid for a few weeks. The sprouts should be potted up into deep pots and moved to a bright spot. Pot on as required. Outdoors the date palm is rather hardy to cold and grows in a range of climates.

Above: Phoenix dactylifera, cultivated, Morocco.

Left: The fruits are the well-known dates.

Phoenix reclinata
Senegal date palm

Features

A well grown Senegal date palm is a wonderful sight. It is a clustering species with several slim stems forming a group. The leaves are a fresh green with orange bases and spines, and the fleshy though barely edible fruits are brown when ripe. It occurs naturally throughout tropical Africa and is often cultivated as an ornamental there. Tolerant of drought and eaten by herbivores at such times, it may be grown in a range of climates. It grows to about 80 feet (25m) in height and the individual trunks are some 12 inches (30cm) in diameter. Poorly grown plants have an untidy appearance.

Cultivation

The seeds should be cleaned of all flesh and given a thorough soak prior to planting in moist peat. In conditions of warmth they will usually sprout in a few weeks and the growth of the seedlings is fast.

Above and right: Phoenix reclinata in habitat, Umfolozi-Hluhluwei Game Reserve, Natal, South Africa.

Phoenix roebelenii
Pigmy date palm

Features

From Laos, on the Mekong Delta in Vietnam, and Yunnan in southern China, comes this beautiful, small species, which has been popular as a house-plant for over a hundred years. It has a slim solitary trunk (clustering in the wild), up to only 4 inches (10cm) or so in diameter and covered with old leaf bases, and a delightful crown of soft, feathery, pinnate leaves, though with spiny leaf bases. The flower stalks are produced from among these and the small flowers are creamy yellow. They go on to bear small inedible oval fruits, which are a dull red-brown when ripe. Male and female flowers are on different plants.

Cultivation

The small seeds germinate easily and quickly, and seedlings grow at a steady rate. Outdoors, these charming palms grow in climates from warm-temperate and Mediterranean to tropical. As houseplants they are unrivaled.

Above: Phoenix roebelenii, cultivated, Fairchild Tropical Garden, Florida, USA.

Right: A clustering form in cultivation at Nong Nooch Garden, Thailand.

A Pocket Guide to Palms

Phoenix rupicola
Cliff date palm

Features

Arguably the most beautiful of all the species in the genus, the Cliff date palm from northern India has a graceful crown of finely divided, feather-shaped leaves that are glossy green. Its slim trunk grows to about 30 feet (10m) in height and the fruits are red when ripe. Seen in its native home on steep hills and cliffs, it presents a striking sight. The fruits are eaten by monkeys. Sadly, it is not much seen in cultivation, but this is certain to change as the seed becomes more widely available.

Cultivation

The small seeds are easy to grow. Mix them when dry with moist peat and keep in the dark in a plastic bag. With warm to hot conditions, they will sprout in a few weeks. Young plants should be potted on as necessary and kept in a bright spot. As a garden tree, it will grow in a range of climates, from warm-temperate to tropical.

Right: Phoenix rupicola, *cultivated, Rangoon, Burma.*

Phoenix sylvestris

Silver date palm

Features

Widely grown across most of India, this solitary species is easily recognized by its spiky plumose leaves, the leaflets radiating in all directions. Sometimes one can drive for miles and see little else but this palm, cultivated by the thousand for the sweet syrup that exudes from cuts made in the upper trunk, which is collected in pots attached to the tree. This can be made into sugar or an alcoholic beverage. The palm grows to about 30 feet (10m) if left untouched, but the continual tapping must surely stunt its growth. The fruits are yellow when ripe and inedible.

Cultivation

Given conditions of moisture and heat, the oval seeds sprout very easily and the seedlings grow quickly. An elegant addition to the tropical garden, it will also grow happily in considerably cooler conditions, and will even tolerate some frost when larger.

Above: Phoenix sylvestris, *cultivated, India.*
Right: Sap is collected from cuts in the trunk, to which bees are also attracted.

A Pocket Guide to Palms

Phoenix theophrastii

Cretan date palm

Features

One of the only two palm species endemic to Europe; the other is *Chamaerops humilis*. It occurs on the island of Crete and in small areas of Turkey, growing in colonies on beaches and rocky, sandy areas. In some places its existence is under threat by hotel development for the tourist trade. It is a suckering species with silvery green foliage and fierce spines on the leaf bases. From among these the flower stalks grow and after flowering produce large clusters of barely edible fruit, brown when ripe.

Cultivation

The seeds germinate easily and quickly and the young plants are fast growing. The extremely tough leaves of this species suggest that it may be rather cold-hardy and it is well worth trying in the temperate garden. Inside it would perform well in the hot, dry conservatory, though its armament may be a detriment to use.

Left: Phoenix theophrasti *in habitat, Vai, Crete.*

Pholidostachys
dactyloides

Features

A beautiful, solitary palm from western Ecuador
and Colombia with striking red new leaves. It
grows to around 26 feet (8m) or more tall with a
slim trunk, and has a fine crown of interesting,
feather-shaped leaves, the leaflets varying in
width. The central ones are red on appearance, later turning to green. This is a key
characteristic, which makes the palm readily
recognizable in the often gloomy rainforest
where it grows at low altitudes. The flower
stalks grow from among the leaves and the
resulting fruits are dark purple when ripe, oval,
and about ⅔ inch (1.5cm) long.

Cultivation

Not much grown in cultivation, it is definitely
one for the hot and humid garden where
there is regular high rainfall. It may be tried as
a houseplant, but it prefers a humid conservatory where the new leaves will certainly
attract attention.

Above: Pholidostachys dactyloides, *Limon to Gualaquiza*
  road, Costa Rica.
Right: The new leaves are dull red.

A Pocket Guide to Palms

Pigafetta filaris
Pigafetta palm

Features

One of the fastest growing of all palms, this solitary species from Sulawesi, the Moluccan Islands, and New Guinea quickly takes advantage of newly created light gaps in the forest and grows rapidly to colonize them. It is a tall tree, growing to perhaps 150 feet (50m), with big, feather-shaped leaves, the spines on their bases forming an interesting and unique pattern. The trunk is green with prominent white rings, the large leaves are arching with the leaflets carried erect, and the inflorescences, which appear among the leaves, go on to produce fruits, strangely small for such a large tree, only ½ inch (1cm) long, and covered with pretty, overlapping scales.

Cultivation

Seeds must be planted within a few days of collection as viability is very short. They germinate fast and the seedlings grow quickly. Becoming more popular, these lovely palms are sometimes seen in tropical botanic gardens.

Above and left: Pigafetta filaris, cultivated, Garrin Fullington Garden, Hawaii.
Far left: The leaf bases are very spiny.

Pinanga coronata
Ivory crownshaft palm

Features

Popular in the tropics, this clumping palm
grows to perhaps 15 feet (5m) tall. The
multiple stems are slim and have a noticeable pale yellow crownshaft. The leaves
themselves are broad, as are the leaflets
which sometimes overlap each other giving
an attractive appearance. It comes from
Indonesia and is essentially a tropical
species, though it is reported that they are able to withstand cool conditions also.
The new leaves are sometimes pink on opening, before turning to green. The
flowerstalk grows from below the crownshaft and the small oval fruits are red.
This makes a lovely palm for the tropical greenhouse or garden.

Cultivation

The small seeds germinate easily and quickly if fresh and the young plants also
grow fast. They should be grown in shade to begin with, later transferred to full sun.

Humid conditions and a rich soil would suit
this palm best.

*Above: Pinanga coronata, cultivated, Singapore Botanic
    Garden.*
Left: Both the fruits and roots are bright red.

Pinanga gracilis

Features

Pinanga is a large genus with well over a hundred species growing, usually as understory palms, in rainforest over a wide range from northern India and across Southeast Asia. This attractive species, with its shiny wet-look leaves, comes from northern India in the foothills of the Himalayas, where it tolerates cool conditions. It is small growing with several thin stems to a clump. The leaves, as may be seen, are rather glossy with chevron-shaped leaflets. The fruits are bright red when ripe, and the shape of an olive.

Cultivation

The small, almond-shaped seeds germinate easily and quickly, and the seedlings grow fast. Given the conditions it requires, those of high humidity, rich soil, and gentle warmth, the young seedlings grow very quickly soon turning into handsome plants. Suitable for the cool and moist conservatory, they will prosper outside given similar conditions.

Left: Pinanga gracilis *in habitat, wet forest, near Kalimpong, W. Bengal, India.*

Plectocomia himalayana

Himalayan rattan palm

Features

A climbing palm from the foothills of the Himalayas, it grows at quite some altitude and endures frost in winter so should be quite cold-hardy. It is a suckering species with canes of just an inch or so in diameter and perhaps 80 feet (25m) in length, which snake upward into the canopy, aided by backward pointing spines that grip

the surrounding foliage. It can often be seen from mountain roads, the leaves appearing among the tree tops. Despite the spines, it is a pretty palm with fine, fresh green, irregularly spaced leaflets. The small round fruits are covered with tiny, attractive, overlapping scales, a greenish-brown when ripe.

Cultivation

The small seeds should be sown fresh and they will germinate easily and quickly. Seedling growth is also rather fast and a good-sized palm can be achieved within a few years.

Left: Plectocomia himalayana, *commonly seen from the roadside near Kalimpong, W. Bengal, India.*

Plectocomia khasiana

Khasi rattan palm

Features

A handsome, even noble, rattan palm that rises in a stately fashion above the surrounding vegetation, its long pendulous leaflets held out on a horizontal rachis as though to be admired. It has a slim, spiny trunk, and is nominally a climbing palm though this may not be obvious when first seen. It grows in the beautiful Khasia Hills of India's Meghalaya Province in the company of *Trachycarpus martianus* and *Wallichia disticha*, in areas of high rainfall, among the highest on earth. The fruits, round to oval and about ¾ inch (2cm) long, are attractively covered with overlapping scales, and yellow-brown when ripe.

Cultivation

An easily grown rattan, it performs well as a houseplant for a few years and the young leaves are extremely pretty and fine. It benefits from humidity in the air and if grown outdoors requires warm conditions in areas of high rainfall.

Above: Plectocomia khasiana, *in habitat, Khasia Hills, Meghalaya Province, India.*
Right: It is seen to perfection in silhouette.

Polyandrococos caudescens
Buri palm

Features

A handsome South American palm with a solitary trunk, frequently seen from the road near the coast of central Brazil. It is often left by farmers when land is cleared for pasture, but whether it is able to reproduce under these conditions is debatable. The height is up to 26 feet (8m), the trunk is about 6 inches (15cm) in diameter and the spreading crown of leaves is held upright with the silvery-white undersides of the leaves clearly visible. Close up, the prettily striped new leaf spears readily confirm its identity. The long, pendulous fruit clusters bear tightly packed fruits, about 1½ inches (4cm) long, brown when ripe. Altogether a nice-looking, smallish palm tree not often seen in cultivation.

Cultivation

The seeds are erratic to germinate and may take from a few weeks to a few months. Once sprouted, the young plants grow steadily. This is a much underused palm, ideal for the tropical garden.

Above: Polyandrococos caudescens, *left in cleared pasture, Espirito Santo, Brazil.*
Right: The curious fruit.

Prestoea acuminata

Features

Surely one of the most widespread rainforest palms in the northwest of South America and Central America, where thousands can be seen in a single day's drive. It has a slim, solitary, or clustering trunk just an inch or so in diameter, a purple crown shaft, and an attractive crown of finely feathered pinnate leaves. Across its wide range, usually on steep slopes, there is much variation, including a choice form which has a red crownshaft, rivaling the red crownshaft palm, *Geonoma undata*, and sometimes growing with it. The small round fruits are about ⅝ inch (1.5cm) in diameter, and purple-black when ripe.

Cultivation

Considering how common it is in the wild it is surprisingly absent in cultivation. The small seeds germinate easily and the seedlings grow fast, so why it is not used

more often is a mystery. It is splendid in the tropical garden, especially in areas of high rainfall.

Above: Prestoea acuminata *in habitat on the "Inca Trail,"*
  Villacabamba, Ecuador.
Left: The bright red petioles.

Pritchardia hillebrandii

Features

One of a genus of about forty species of handsome fan palms, for many the very essence of the tropics. Most grow in the Hawaiian Islands, some on totally inaccessible mountaintops, and many are endangered in the wild and may only survive in cultivation. This species grows to about 20 feet (6m) in height, the trunk is smooth and solitary and bears a crown of big, fresh-green, or blue-green, fan-shaped leaves. The petioles are covered with a woolly substance, the inflorescences grow among the leaves and after flowering produce round fruits about ¾ inch (2cm) in diameter, black and glossy when ripe.

Cultivation

Some *Pritchardia* are difficult to grow; this species is among the easiest. The seeds are easy to obtain, and germinate within a few weeks, the seedlings grow fast and without problems. It is wonderful for the humid conservatory or, of course, for the tropical and subtropical garden.

Above and right: Pritchardia hillebrandii,
cultivated, National Tropical Botanical
Garden, Kalaheo, Kauai, Hawaii.
Far right: The leaf bases are covered in white
tomentum.

A Pocket Guide to Palms

Pritchardia pacifica
Fiji fan palm

Features

One of the few in the genus not to come from Hawaii though it was probably introduced into Fiji. Perhaps the most widely planted *Pritchardia*, it is a large, unmistakable, and attractive tropical palm with stiff, upright, fan-shaped leaves held erect. The segments are many and fine, the trunk, growing up to about 30 feet (10m), is slim and covered with old leaf bases, especially near the top. A group of these palms is a stunning sight indeed. The flowers grow among the leaves and the small, round fruits, black when ripe, are produced in abundance.

Cultivation

Although the small round seeds germinate easily, under glass the young seedlings are much more difficult and seem prone to yellowing and attacks by spider mite, so a careful watch should be kept on them. As the plants grow, so they become more reliable. In the tropics, at least, they are fast growing and soon reach maturity.

Left: Pritchardia pacifica, *cultivated, Marriott Beach Resort, Kauai, Hawaii.*

Pseudophoenix lediniana

Features

Pseudophoenix is a small genus of just a few species of remarkable feather-leaved palms from the Caribbean. This wonderful tall palm from just one valley in Haiti is very rare in the wild. Its solitary, spindle-shaped, prominently ringed trunk, bulging slightly in the middle and at the base, is dark green and waxy. It carries an open crown of stiff arching leaves with glossy leaflets. The inflorescences arise from among the leaves and become pendulous with the weight of the fruits. These are round, about ¾ inch (2cm) in diameter, and red-brown when ripe.

Cultivation

Much patience is required to grow these attractive palms. The seeds are erratic to germinate and subsequent seedling growth is extremely slow. It may be many years before a trunk begins to show. Suited to tropical climates and tolerant of coastal exposure.

Left: Pseudophoenix lediniana, *cultivated, Fairchild Tropical Garden, Florida, USA.*

Pseudophoenix sargentii
Cherry palm

Features

From a wide area of the Caribbean, extending up into the tip of Florida, this is probably the best known of this little seen genus. It is a slim palm, which grows to about 26 feet (8m) tall, and the ringed trunk, bearing the scars of fallen leaves, is covered with a thin layer of wax. It may be enlarged at the base. The stiff, feather-shaped leaves rise in an open crown, glossy green above and silvery white beneath. The most attractive feature is the great clusters of bright red cherry-like fruits, which grow on inflorescences appearing among the leaves and becoming pendulous.

Cultivation

Extremely slow growing, which accounts for its rarity in cultivation. However, professional nurserymen in Florida are a patient lot and plants of this species are beginning to be seen more widely for sale. A tropical or subtropical climate suits it best, and it is tolerant of salt spray.

Above: Pseudophoenix sargentii, *cultivated, Fairchild Tropical Garden, Florida, USA.*
Above right: The yellow flowers are fragrant.
Right: The small fruits are bright red.

Pseudophoenix vinifera

Buccaneer palm

Features

The common name evokes visions of Caribbean islands and pirates, appropriate for this curious palm that comes from Haiti and the Dominican Republic. It grows on limestone hillsides in areas where rainfall is very low, and this may account for its extremely swollen trunk, which is unmistakable. The leaves are stiff, upright and arching, silvery green, and all parts of the tree have a thin layer of whitish wax. The spectacular fruit clusters are bright red when ripe and

hang down from among the leaves. This, together with the unusual moody green-blue of the foliage, leaves a lasting impression.

Cultivation

Again, much patience is required before this special palm gets to any size. Buying an established plant from the specialist nursery will save years, though may be expensive. From seed, growth is extremely slow. Dry tropical conditions suit it best.

Above: Pseudophoenix vinifera, *cultivated, Montgomery Botanical Center, Florida, USA.*
Left: The fruit clusters are bright red when ripe.

Ptychosperma macarthurii
Macarthur palm

Features

The most popular and widespread member of a genus of about thirty species, it is a slim, clustering palm with narrow stems to about 25 feet (8m) in height. The trunks are attractively ringed and carry a neat crown of pinnate feathery leaves, held upright and arching, with slightly jagged leaflet tips. Inflorescences grow from below the crownshaft and after flowering produce clusters of bright red fruits, ½ inch (1cm) or so long. Each fruit contains a seed, which has about five ridges along its length, a key identification characteristic for *Ptychosperma*. This species comes from north east Australia and New Guinea, but is widely planted in the tropics generally.

Cultivation

Very easy and satisfying to grow, the seeds require warmth and humidity in moist peat and sprout rather quickly if planted fresh. The seedlings also grow rather fast given rich soil and plenty of water. A splendid small palm for the tropical garden.

Left: Ptychosperma macarthurii, *cultivated, Hilo Zoo, Hawaii.*

Raphia australis
Raphia palm

Features

This impressive palm, one of about thirty in the genus, has characteristically long leaves, among the longest in the entire vegetable kingdom. They can be up to 66 feet (20m) in length and were formerly used for the manufacture of raphia string, though the use of this has lessened as manmade materials take over. It occurs in southern Africa, "australis" meaning "south," and is generally found in swampy areas. The leaf petioles are orange and may be rather spiny. The trunk is solitary and grows to about 20 feet (7m) tall and the extraordinary flower stalk, which itself can be about 8 feet (2 or 3m) long, hangs down from among the leaves. After flowering it goes on to produce large, round, fruits, covered in scales. Each trunk dies after fruiting.

Cultivation

The large oval seeds, up to about 2½ inches (6cm) long, need very wet and warm conditions to germinate and are slow and erratic. The resulting seedlings grow very fast. Best grown in the large park or garden where its size can be appreciated, it requires swampy conditions to thrive.

Right: Raphia australis, *cultivated, Floribunda Nursery, Hilo, Hawaii.*

Ravenea hildebrandtii

Features

A rare and beautiful small palm (one of about twenty in the genus), from the Comoro Islands off the northwest coast of Madagascar, where it grows in wet forest. It is also rare in cultivation though seeds have recently appeared on the market. It has a slim, solitary trunk to maybe 20 feet (7m) in height and 3 or 4 inches (about 12 cm) or so across, which is enlarged at the base. The feather-shaped grass-green leaves are held in an upright, neat crown. The inflorescences are pendulous and after flowering produce round to oval fruits about ½ inch (1cm) in diameter,

which hang down from among the leaves. The fruits are a bright orange when ripe.

Cultivation

This charming small palm deserves to be more widely grown and hopefully will be as seed becomes more available. It requires tropical or subtropical conditions and an abundance of water. The small round seeds germinate within a few weeks.

Left: Ravenea hillebrandii, *cultivated, Montgomery Botanical Center, Florida.*

Ravenea rivularis

Majesty palm

Features

This useful Madagascan palm has risen from total obscurity to worldwide popularity in the space of a few years and is now grown by the million for chainstore use. It is a fast growing, stout trunked palm with an attractive crown of grass-green, soft, feathery pinnate leaves. The trunk grows to about 80 feet (25m) tall and some 24 inches (60cm) in diameter, is pale brown, rather soft, and easily damaged. The inflorescences rise from among the leaves and produce large amounts of small round fruits, which are red when ripe.

Cultivation

Seeds are exported from Madagascar by the million for the houseplant industry. They sprout quickly and seedling growth is very fast. They prefer damp conditions, and an adequate supply of water will certainly aid growth. Outside they prefer tropical or subtropical conditions and grow very quickly once planted. They make excellent indoor subjects that are happiest in bright light.

Right: Ravenea rivularis, *cultivated, Fairchild Tropical Garden, Florida, USA.*

Reinhardtia gracilis

Windowpane palm

Features

A delightful small palm found widely across Central America where it grows in rainforests. The slim trunks are solitary or clustered, up to only 6½ feet (2m) in height and ⅗ inch (1.5cm) across. The few dark green and glossy, pinnate leaves have broad, widely spaced, wedge-shaped leaflets each with a number of holes or slots ("windowpanes") near the base. The tips are squared off and toothed. The inflorescences arise among the leaves and after flowering produce small quantities of oval fruits, ½ inch (1 cm) or so long, purple to black when ripe.

Cultivation

These palms have achieved some popularity as houseplants because of their dainty appearance, but they are not easy to either grow or maintain. They seem fussy

about air humidity and require rich soil and regular watering. Outside they are appropriate for moist tropical and sub-tropical locations and prefer shade.

Above: Reinhardtia gracilis, *in habitat, Cordillera Guanacaste, Costa Rica.*

Left: The small "windows" in the leaves give the palm its name.

Rhapidophyllum hystrix

Needle palm

Features

With the distinction of being the world's hardiest palm, it is capable of surviving an incredible –4°F (–20 °C). It is a low growing, suckering species from southeastern USA, with glossy fan-shaped leaves, and leaflets that spread like fingers. It occurs in damp forests, does not grow much of a trunk, and the entire plant rarely exceeds 6½ feet (2m) in height. The trunk that is produced is covered with sharp, upward pointing, black spines that make seed collecting rather interesting. The flowers are produced among the leaf bases and the fruits that follow are about ½ inch (1cm) in diameter, round, and brown when ripe.

Cultivation

Grown mainly as a curiosity, this hardy palm grows very slowly in cool climates and is much happier in the subtropical garden. It can be grown from seed but it is a slow process.

Above: Rhapidophyllum hystrix, *in habitat, Highlands Hammock State Park, Florida, USA.*
Left: The black spines are very sharp.

A Pocket Guide to Palms

Rhapis excelsa
Lady palm

Features

Rhapis are delightful small palms originating in China and Southeast Asia, where they grow in dry forests. *R. excelsa* is one in a genus of some 12 species, and all seem ideally suitable as houseplants, tolerating very low light. It is a suckering species with a number of slim, fibrous canes and only about ½ inch (1cm) in diameter. The height of the plant is only up to about 10 feet (3m), despite the scientific name, and it bears an open crown of dark green, glossy fan leaves that

have widely spread segments like fingers, with notched tips. The flowers grow among the leaves and the fruits are small, oval, and black when ripe.

Cultivation

It makes one of the very best houseplants, as it tolerates very low light and general neglect. The small seeds germinate well but grow slowly. The plant may also be increased by splitting the clump. Excellent in the tropical or temperate garden.

Left: Rhapis excelsa, *cultivated, Singapore Botanic Garden.*

Rhapis humilis
Slender lady palm

Features

This palm is found naturally in south China where it grows in open forests. Despite the scientific name, it can grow higher than *R. excelsa* and clumps of 13 feet (4m) tall are not uncommon. The leaflets are slimmer than *R. excelsa* and the whole plant presents a finer appearance. The stems are rather slim, up to just ½ inch (1cm) or so in diameter and they are covered in fine fibrous netting. Each leaf has around fifteen leaflets, slim and pointed with slightly toothed tips. The male flowers are produced on short flower stalks among the leaves.

Cultivation

Interestingly, only male plants of this species are known in cultivation and propagation must be done by division. This can be done by carefully separating a clump into two halves. Pull the roots apart trying to do the minimum of damage, though some roots may have to be cut. Pot up each half and, after a short recovery period, they should carry on growing without setback.

Right: Rhapis humilis, *cultivated, Royal Botanic Garden, Kew, England.*

A Pocket Guide to Palms

Rhapis multifida

Features

This fine-leaved *Rhapis* is gradually being seen more as seed and plants become available. It comes from southern China where it may be found growing wild in open groups in forested regions, where it grows to only about 6½ feet (2m) tall. The stems are less than ½ inch (1cm) in diameter and the leaflets, the narrowest of any *Rhapis*, may be less than ½ inch (1cm) wide. This gives the entire plant a fine, delicate look. Both male and female flowers are produced on short flower stalks held among the leaves. The small round fruits are less than ½ inch (1cm) in diameter and black when ripe.

Cultivation

Seeds of this wonderfully decorative small palm are becoming more widely and regularly available and it is hoped that the plants will be more frequently seen as a result. They should be planted in moist peat and kept warm in the dark. Germination occurs within a few weeks but the seedlings grow slowly.

Above: Rhapis multifida, *cultivated, Kunming, Yunnan, China.*
Right: The finely cut leaf.

Rhopalostylis baueri
Norfolk Island palm

Features

This small genus of attractive Australasian palms contains just a few species. *R. baueri* is a handsome tree with stiff, upright, feather-shaped leaves above a bulging crownshaft. They are sometimes called shuttlecock or shaving brush palms for this reason. They occur naturally in forested areas on Norfolk Island. The leaves are dark green and they, and the leaf bases, are covered with a pale brown tomentum. The trunk is slim and prominently ringed and grows to about 50 feet (15m) tall. The inflorescences arise below the crownshaft and produce ¾ inch (2cm) long, olive-like fruits, reddish brown when ripe.

Cultivation

The round seeds germinate erratically; subsequent seedling growth is steady. An excellent contender for gardens in warm-temperate climates, where they grow slowly. They make good houseplants while young.

Above: Rhopalostylis baueri, *cultivated, Balboa Park, CA, USA.*
Right: The crownshaft and inflorescence.

Rhopalostylis sapida

Shaving brush or Nikau palm

Features

A beefed-up version of *R. baueri*, with a thicker trunk, smaller crownshaft but broader leaflets. They grow in moist forest all over the North Island of New Zealand and on the west coast of the South Island in dense colonies. It is the most southerly-growing palm in the world. The leaves are held stiff and upright, there is a noticeable crownshaft, sometimes bulging, and the trunk, up to about 40 feet (12m) only, is ringed with the scars of fallen leaves. The flowerstalks grow from below the crownshaft, the flowers are purple-mauve, and the fruits that follow flowering are bright red when ripe.

Cultivation

Sometimes considered as having some resistance to cold, they will only tolerate a few degrees of frost. They will, however, grow slowly but steadily in cool climates so may be suitable for temperate gardens given some protection during the coldest months.

Above: Rhopalostylis sapida, cultivated, Balboa Park, CA, USA.
Left: The bulging crownshaft.

Roystonea oleracae

Venezuelan royal palm

Features

Perhaps the most impressive of all palms, royals (there are ten in the genus) are usually tall and stout with trunks like marble columns. This one, from Venezuela, Colombia, and some offshore islands, is the tallest of all, at up to an incredible 130 feet (40m). The almost white trunk is about 20 inches (50cm) in diameter. There is a prominent grass-green crownshaft, above which the handsome feather leaves are held horizontally, resulting in a rather flat crown. The flowerstalks are huge and appear immediately below the crownshaft, or rather, are revealed as the leafbase that covers them falls away. The small round seeds follow white flowers and are bright red when ripe.

Cultivation

The small seeds are produced in large numbers and are easy to germinate. Young plants grow quickly but it is nonetheless some years before a trunk is produced. Suitable for the tropical garden, these long-lived palms would be a valuable addition.

Above: Roystonea oleracae, cultivated, Caracas Botanical Garden, Venezuela.

Left: Roystonea oleracae make an imposing avenue. Venezuela.

A Pocket Guide to Palms

Roystonea regia
Cuban or Florida royal palm

Features

Grows in the wild from Cuba across to Central America and just touching the southern tip of Florida, in swampy districts or in disturbed areas. Its whitish trunk grows up to 100 feet (30m) by about 20 inches (50cm) across. The fresh green pinnate leaves are slightly plumose in appearance, the flowerstalk juts out below the prominent green crown shaft, and the flowers are white. The resultant fruits are small, round, bright red when ripe, and grow in huge numbers. It is an impressive sight with its crown appearing above the surrounding vegetation in the Florida everglades.

Cultivation

The small round seeds germinate easily and quickly and the young seedlings grow fast. Within a few years they produce a trunk and even large trees may be only 10 or 20 years old. Frequently seen in botanic gardens all over the tropics and subtropics.

Above: Roystonea regia, *cultivated, Fairchild Tropical Garden, Florida, USA.*
Right: Royal Palm Avenue, Singapore Botanic Garden.

Palms

Sabal causiarum

Puerto Rican hat palm

Features

Sabal is a genus of sixteen species, occurring on Caribbean Islands and on the surrounding mainland, where they are widespread, well-known, and sometimes extremely common. This species grows in Haiti and Puerto Rico near the coast on sandy soils. It may be distinguished by its massive trunk, only to about 30 feet (10m) in height but up to 30 inches (70cm) in diameter. The large fan-shaped leaves are stiff, with thick petioles, forming a dense and spherical crown. The flowerstalks appear among the leaves and extend beyond them. After flowering they produce clusters of round fruit, about ½ inch (1cm) in diameter, black when ripe.

Cultivation

The small round seeds are easy to grow, and germinate quickly. Seedling growth is steady and it takes but a short time to produce the trunk. These huge palms are best grown in the ground in a tropical garden or park where their great size can best be appreciated.

Right: Sabal causiarum, *cultivated, Fairchild Tropical Garden, Florida, USA.*

Sabal mauritiiformis

Features

An unusual *Sabal*, from the north of South America and with a separate population in Mexico, its leaves are much more open than all other species and have pendulous tips, giving it a unique, if untidy, appearance. It is named for its apparent similarity to *Mauritia* and there is some resemblance. The trunk grows to some 50 feet (15m) tall, is slimmer than other species, and the inflorescences appear among the leaves and extend beyond them. The small fruits, up to about ½ inch (1cm) long, are round and black when ripe. They are often left by farmers when woodland is cleared for pasture, though whether they reproduce in these conditions is debatable since the cattle are likely to eat the young seedlings.

Cultivation

Germinate the seeds in the usual way in moist peat. Maintain the warmth and they should sprout in just a few weeks. Easy, but slow to put on any size.

Left: Sabal mauritiiformis, *in habitat, Huixtla, Mexico.*

Sabal mexicana

Features

Occurring in coastal southern Mexico and adjacent countries, this distinctive palm grows in enormous colonies and can be seen for miles in every direction from certain vantage points. The leaves are big, fan-shaped, and strongly costapalmate. The trunk grows to about 50 feet (15m) and is often covered with old leaf bases, making an interesting pattern. The flowerstalks grow among the leaves and are followed by

big clusters of black fruits, ⅔ inch (1.5cm) long. Small buildings and huts are sometimes thatched with the dried leaves of this palm, and the heart is apparently edible. This is perhaps one of the most common palms in the world.

Cultivation

This palm is surprisingly rare in cultivation when its abundance in the wild is considered. The small round seeds sprout easily and the young plants grow quite fast, so why it is not more widely grown is a mystery.

Left: Sabal mexicana, *in cleared pasture, San Luis Potosi, Mexico.*

Sabal minor
Dwarf palmetto palm

Features

A well-known and popular small palm, famous for its ability to withstand very low temperatures, doubtless it is one of the world's most cold-hardy species. Found growing in swamps in southern and southeastern USA, it usually does not grow a trunk, or at least no more than a subterranean one. However, some individuals with

trunks are known. The blue-green leaves are costapalmate and split into two halves. The petioles are strong and the leaves are held upright. The inflorescences are upright also, and extend beyond the leaves. These bear fruit, which are about ½ inch (1cm) in diameter, and black when ripe.

Cultivation

Though undoubtedly very hardy to cold, this nice palm grows very slowly in temperate countries. It is better able to withstand occasional bitter cold rather than continual cool conditions, though it is certainly worth trying in sheltered areas, perhaps in a sunny corner.

Left: Sabal minor, *in habitat, Highlands Hammock State Park, Florida, USA.*

Sabal palmetto

Palmetto palm

Features

This is the state tree of Florida, where it is extremely common, growing by the hundred thousand in vast colonies from horizon to horizon in some areas. It is also very widely used as a street tree there and in shopping malls, and tens of thousands are extracted from the wild (apparently without ill effects either to the palm itself or to the population) every year. It is a handsome species with a spherical crown of costapalmate, blue-green leaves, growing atop a stout trunk to perhaps 50 or 60 feet (15 or 20m) in height. The small round fruits, which are black when ripe, are produced in abundance and cover the ground under the tree when they fall.

Cultivation

A very easy palm to grow though it is slow to form any kind of trunk. The small round seeds sprout easily given a little heat and humidity and the seedlings grow at a respectable rate.

Right: Sabal palmetto, *popular as a street tree, Florida, USA.*

A Pocket Guide to Palms

Sabal uresana
Palma blanca ("white palm")

Features

Grows in a comparatively small area in northwest Mexico, but is rather common within its limited range. This is another example of an attractive palm, common enough in the wild and inexplicably rare in cultivation. Small plants change hands for

hundreds of dollars. Palma blanca grows a tall solitary trunk to around 65 feet (20m) tall or more but its distinguishing feature is that the leaves are a silvery blue, most noticeable in young plants but still apparent in mature specimens. From a distance they can indeed look almost white. The fruit stalks grow among the leaves and after flowering produce small, slightly oval fruits, which are black when ripe and about ⅗ inch (1.5cm) long.

Cultivation

Efforts should be made to introduce this beautiful and unusual species more widely into cultivation. The seeds are produced in large quantities and grow fast and easily.

Left: Sabal uresana, *in habitat, Bahia San Carlos, Mexico.*

Serenoa repens

Saw palmetto

Features

From the southeast of the USA, this short but pretty palm is extremely common and colonies can easily be seen from the car on many of the roads in some areas. The trunk is short or prostrate and creeping, sometimes underground. The leaves are fan-shaped and stiff and the leaf stalks thorny (hence the "saw" of the common name). The leaf varies from green through blue-green to blue-silver. The more

choice examples are sought after as landscape plants. The slim trunks, which grow to a maximum of 10 feet (3m) tall, bear flowerstalks among the leaves. After flowering these produce fruits, which are oval and about ¾ inch (2cm) long, and black when ripe. The seeds are collected in vast numbers for use in medicine, which already may be having an effect on this palm's regeneration, as is the continued clearance of its habitat for house building.

Cultivation

Large plants seen for sale are likely to have been removed from the wild. They are easy, but slow, to grow from seed.

Top: Serenoa repens, common in Florida, USA. Green and blue forms co-exist.
Above: The beautiful silver-blue form of this species.
Right: The inflorescence, about to flower.

A Pocket Guide to Palms

Socratea exorrhiza

Features

A splendid, up to 70 feet (20m), slim, solitary palm from the northern half of South America where it is locally common, often seen as a sloping "cross" on distant ridge tops. The trunk, which has a long crownshaft, is about 6 inches (15cm) in diameter and is supported on older trees by stilt roots, which grow from above ground level

and stabilize the tree. Epiphytes sometimes grow on the trunk. The leaves are strongly plumose with distinctive pendulous tips, and the inflorescences grow from below the crownshaft, producing round fruits about 1 inch (3cm) in diameter, in large clusters, which are yellow-brown when ripe.

Cultivation

The marble-sized seeds germinate easily and seedlings grow at a satisfactory rate. It is suitable as a conservatory plant, otherwise it requires warm, moist, and humid conditions in rich soil and is not much seen as a cultivated plant in its native land.

Left: Socratea exorrhiza, *cultivated, Jardin Botanico Robert y Catherine Wilson, Puntarenas, Costa Rica.*

Syagrus botryophora

Features

Syagrus is a big genus of some thirty species, which grow all over South America. This one is usually seen by the roadside as an isolated tree, or in small groups in coastal eastern Brazil. It is tall, growing up to about 65 feet (20m), with a slim trunk about 8 inches (20cm) in diameter, and has a lovely crown of arching, pinnate, glossy green leaves. The flowering stem is produced among the leaves, concealed within a long, grooved, woody "bract," which falls away revealing the flowers. This is a characteristic of the genus. The fruits are ellipsoid, about 1 inch (3cm) in diameter, and yellow-orange when ripe.

Cultivation

The ellipsoid seeds germinate after some weeks or months and seedling growth is very fast. Even so, this attractive palm is not often seen in cultivation, which is a great pity. Suitable for warm-temperate to tropical regions.

Above: Syagrus botryophora, *in habitat, Espirito Santo, Brazil.*
Right: The bract is opening, revealing the flowers.

Syagrus duartei

Features

Not often seen, this short and small palm would be wonderful in the botanic garden. It originates from Minas Gerais in Brazil and the slim, solitary trunk grows only to about 10 feet (3m) in height and is covered with old leaf bases and scars. The blue-green leaves are very stiff and about 3 feet (1m) in length. The segments are held upright and the general appearance is one of a hard and tough

palm, which it undoubtedly is. The ¾ inch (2cm) diameter round fruits are produced on pendulous fruiting branches, which hang out and down with the weight. They are brownish when ripe and have a rough surface.

Cultivation

It is a great pity that this jaunty palm is not more widely grown. Certainly the seeds do not germinate easily or quickly, neither is seedling growth anything other than unreasonably slow. Even so, it is hoped that some enterprising nursery will take the plunge and start producing them in large numbers.

Above: Syagrus duartei, in habitat, Minas Gerais, Brazil.

Right: The round fruits are brown when ripe.

Syagrus flexuosa
Coco de campo

Features

From open woodland and cleared areas in southeast and central Brazil, this is one of the few suckering species of *Syagrus*. This unusual palm has a number of slim stems, which grow to about 15 feet (5m) in height, and are about 3 inches (8cm) in diameter, sometimes covered in old leaf bases. The soft, finely divided pinnate leaves are somewhat plumose. The inflorescences arise among the leaves and hang down with the weight of the fruits, which are brown when ripe, slightly oval, and about 1 inch (3cm) long.

Cultivation

This palm is rarely seen outside its native country. The seeds are tricky to germinate and may do so erratically over a period of months. Seedlings grow very slowly. Definitely one for the tropical or subtropical garden or, as a young plant, in the conservatory.

Above: Syagrus flexuosa, *in habitat, Minas Gerais, Brazil.*

Syagrus glaucescens

Features

From a comparatively small area in eastern Brazil, this stiff-looking species is famously seen on the Diamantina road, growing among rounded boulders in some quantities. The trunk grows to some 13 feet (4m) in height and the leaf bases immediately beneath the crown are formed into five ranks. The blue-green leaves are stiff, pinnate, upwardly pointing and the leaflets are closely spaced. The general appearance is one of a stiff and hard palm, which looks wind and weatherproof. The rounded fruits form after the flowers have fallen, on inflorescences which hang down from among the leaves. The fruits are about ¾ inch (2cm) in diameter, yellow initially and finally brown when ripe.

Cultivation

This would be a wonderful palm for anyone's collection. However, it would be extremely slow growing (though probably faster than in the wild where it experiences tough conditions). The small, conical seeds germinate erratically and the young plants grow slowly.

Above: Syagrus glaucescens, in habitat, Minas Gerais, Brazil.
Left: The rounded fruits form after the flowers.

Syagrus macrocarpa

Features

This rare palm was thought to be extinct and may indeed be on the verge of extinction in its home in southeastern Brazil. A few scattered individuals are to be seen from the road on farmland. They are left after clearance for pasture, but they are unlikely to reproduce after this as cattle undoubtedly eat the young plants. They grow to about 25 feet (8m) tall, the leaves are slightly plumose, and the trunk is smooth, ringed, and bare. The inflorescences hang down from among the leaves and the fruits are the size of hen's eggs, oval, and about 3 inches (7cm) long, which is huge for *Syagrus*.

Cultivation

There are a few trees of this species in botanic gardens and it is from these that seed is sometimes available. Any effort to grow this rare palm should be made in case the few wild trees left die out never to be replaced.

Right: Syagrus macrocarpa, *semi-cultivated, Espirito Santo, Brazil.*

Syagrus romanzoffiana
Queen palm

Features

A popular street tree in many tropical and subtropical countries, they are cultivated in nurseries by the hundred thousand for municipal decoration. Because they are widely grown, they are widely available, which increases their cultivation even more. This over use is a shame as there are many other species, which would perform just as well, that are not even considered by most growers. This situation will surely change. Queen palm grows to about 50 feet (15m) tall and occurs widely in southeastern Brazil and the edge of adjacent countries. It is a handsome tree with a wide and spreading crown of long and graceful, plumose leaves. The fruit stalks hang down from among the leaves and produce great quantities of bright orange fleshy fruit, which is round, and about an inch (2.5cm) in diameter.

Cultivation

This palm is easy in all respects and performs well in gardens from tropical to temperate climates.

Left: Syagrus romanzoffiana, *semi-cultivated, with Pico de Orizaba in the background, Vera Cruz, Mexico.*

Syagrus sancona
Sumunqué

Features

A splendid *Syagrus* from the west of northern South America where it grows on the Andes foothills and surrounding areas, in open forest and cleared pasture. The tall trunk can grow up to 100 feet (30m) in height and is slim. The compact crown is tight, neat, and spherical, and the leaves are markedly plumose giving the tree a distinctive, handsome appearance. The inflorescences arise among the leaves and are protected initially with a woody bract, which falls away in due course, revealing the creamy white flowers. These are followed by large clusters of slightly oval fruits, about ¾ inch (2cm) long, and yellow-orange when ripe.

Cultivation

Not much known outside its habitat, this would be a wonderful palm for street decoration in countries with climates from temperate to tropical. It is easily grown, though the seeds are hard to germinate and this can take some weeks or months.

Right: Syagrus sancona, *in habitat, Ecuador.*

Syagrus werdermannii

Features

Most *Syagrus* are tree palms, some growing to great heights. However, there are a few species that do not form any appreciable trunk. This unusual, low growing, clustering *Syagrus* with stems absent or below ground, is commonly seen by the roadside in one comparatively small area of eastern Brazil where it forms colonies on sandy soil. The blue-green leaves are held upright and grow to about 5 feet (1.5m) long, and the leaflets are stiff and upward pointing. The inflorescences arise from among the leaves and are erect. Flowering is followed by upright clusters of oval fruits, the size and shape of large olives, which are yellow-green when ripe.

Cultivation

Almost unknown outside its homeland, it would make an interesting addition to any collection, public or private. The seeds germinate erratically and subsequent seedling growth is slow. Suitable for a range of climates, temperate to subtropical.

Above: Syagrus werdermanii, *in habitat, Minas Gerais, Brazil.*
Right: Young, unripe fruits.

Thrinax morrisii

Brittle thatch palm

Features

This pretty fan palm is one in a small genus of just six species that grow in the Caribbean Islands and extreme southern Florida. Restricted to the Keys area in Florida, Brittle thatch palm has a solitary trunk, which grows to about 30 feet (10m) tall. The circular, fan-shaped leaves are glossy green above and silvery white below, showing off wonderfully in the slightest breeze. The inflorescences grow from among the leaves, arching out beyond them, and produce round fruits, less than ½ inch (1cm) in diameter, white when ripe.

Cultivation

The small round seeds are widely available and germinate easily, though subsequent seedling growth is slow. Large plants of this species seen for sale in Florida may well have been taken from the wild. Makes a good tub plant in tropical or subtropical climates and a useful conservatory subject too, tolerating great heat and dry air.

Right: Thrinax morrisii, *cultivated, Fairchild Tropical Garden, Florida, USA.*

Thrinax radiata
Thatch palm

Features

This palm may be seen on the Florida Keys where it grows in sandy scrubland. It also occurs across a wide area of the western Caribbean into Central America and Mexico. It has a very slim trunk, only 4 or 5 inches (10 or 12cm) in diameter, and grows to some 30 feet (10m) tall. The big fan-shaped leaves are green on both upper and lower surfaces. The flower stalks are long and arching, forming among the leaves, but not extending beyond them. The resulting fruits are small, round, and white when ripe. They are produced in large quantities.

Cultivation

Patience is required to grow these attractive palms. Although the seeds germinate within a few weeks, the young plants grow very slowly and it is a number of years

before any trunk is seen. It is a pretty palm for the tropical garden but also a suitable interior palm for the hot, dry, and bright conservatory.

Above: Thrinax radiata, *in habitat, Cayo Largo, Cuba.*
Left: The pretty fruits are white when ripe.

Trachycarpus fortunei

Chusan palm

Features

This is one of the most popular cultivated palms in the world, at least in temperate regions, where its cold hardiness is legendary. Cultivated for hundreds of years in China its precise origins are unknown but are assumed to be in central and northern China. It has a solitary, fibrous trunk, which in China at least is stripped off for brushes, brooms, door mats, and even a crude kind of rain cape. The leaves are fan-shaped, about 3 feet (1m) across, the fruits are kidney shaped, about ½ inch (1cm) long, and blue-black when ripe. Male and female are on separate trees.

Cultivation

The seeds germinate easily without heat in four to six weeks and seedling growth is moderate. Suitable for a wide range of climates, it can tolerate temperatures as low as 5°F (–15°C), and is therefore one of the most cold-tolerant palms in the world.

Above: Trachycarpus fortunei, *cultivated, Germany.*
Left: The yellow flowers, just about to open.

Trachycarpus geminisectus

Features

An only recently discovered palm that is yet to be described (publication in preparation), and like so many others in the genus is found growing in an apparently very small territory, an indication that there may well be more species just waiting to be found. Growing on steep hillsides in Ha Giang Province in North Vietnam close to the Chinese border, one of its main distinguishing characteristics is that the leaf segments are fused together in pairs along their length, a feature unique in the genus. The scientific name means "twin-segments." They seem to be quite rare and are rather scattered, so whether they will ever make it into cultivation is debatable. The fruits are kidney-shaped, and the trunk is fibrous.

Cultivation

As yet, nothing is known of its cultivation requirements, but they are likely to be as for other species in the genus.

Above: Trachycarpus geminisectus, *in habitat, Bat Dai Son, Ha Giang Province, North Vietnam.*
Right: The twinned leaflets are seen clearly in this young plant.

Trachycarpus latisectus
Windamere palm

Features

Originally known from only two trees outside the famous Windamere Hotel in Darjeeling, India, it was later found to be growing in some numbers in the gardens of nearby Kalimpong. After a thorough search, it was finally tracked down to a small wild population not far from there, and was described as a new species in 1998. *Latisectus* means "broad segment," referring to its most distinctive characteristic. The trunk is bare, the leaves fan-shaped, and the seeds resemble coffee beans, oval and grooved, yellow to blue-black when ripe.

Cultivation

This attractive palm should be more widely grown as it would be a wonderful addition to any warm-temperate garden. The seeds germinate readily and the seedlings grow very quickly, soon showing character leaves with their unique broad segments. They do not transplant well and care should be taken when moving them.

Above: Trachycarpus latisectus
in habitat, Mirik Busty,
Kalimpong, W. Bengal, India.
Left: The oval fruits each contain
a grooved seed.
Right: The yellow flowers on a
tree in the wild.

A Pocket Guide to Palms

Trachycarpus martianus

Martius' fan palm

Features

A beautiful and elegant *Trachycarpus* from two distinct populations, one at 5,000 feet (1,500m) in the Khasia Hills, Meghalaya Province, northeast India, the other at 8,000 feet (2,400m) in central northern Nepal. There may well be other populations. The main identifying characteristics are the regular leaf splits (to about half way), the coffee bean shaped seeds and the bare, as opposed to fibrous, trunk. The new leaf spear and edges of the petioles are covered with a white tomentum.

Cultivation

The oval seeds germinate easily and seedling growth is quite steady. The seedlings seem to be attractive to pests, so a watchful eye should be kept for red spider mite and mealy bug. Contrary to popular belief, these palms grow on acid soil rather than limestone so will benefit from the use of the appropriate medium. They are only moderately hardy to cold, though will tolerate an occasional light frost.

Above: Trachycarpus martianus *in habitat, Marsyandi Valley, Nepal.*

Right: These yellow fruits will be blue-black when fully ripe.

Trachycarpus nanus

Yunnan dwarf palm

Features

Unique in the genus, *T. nanus* has only an underground or shortly emergent trunk. It covers a wide area in western China (Yunnan Province) but is alas regularly predated by domestic goats, which range far and wide eating anything in their path. The fan leaves, which are deeply split, are held upright, as are the flowers and fruits, which are kidney-shaped and bluish black when ripe. The leaf varies from dark green to an attractive blue-silver. Efforts should be made to conserve this pretty little palm as it is threatened in the wild. It occurs both in open forest and in pasture.

Cultivation

The seeds germinate readily enough, but the seedlings grow very slowly and it will be a few years before character leaves are seen. It is very cold-hardy and would be a welcome addition to the temperate garden.

Above right: Trachycarpus nanus in habitat and under threat, Yunnan Province, China.

Above: The kidney-shaped fruits.

Trachycarpus oreophilus

Thai mountain palm

Features

Growing in some numbers but in a comparatively small mountainous area of northern Thailand, *T. oreophilus* was thought to be a form of *Livistona* until its true identity was discovered and it was published as a new species. The trunk is slim and bare, sometimes lichen covered, the leaves irregularly fan-shaped, and the seeds kidney-shaped and blue-black when ripe. In its mountain home, at over 6,500 feet (2,000m), it is intermittently covered by cloud and grows in pockets of soil among the rocks. Formerly more common than now, it has been cut down for building materials.

Cultivation

Some seeds have been introduced into cultivation. These have proved to germinate within a few weeks, though seedling growth is slow and character leaves do not appear for several years. Due to the inaccessibility of the native populations, it is doubtful whether this attractive palm will ever make it into general cultivation.

Above: Trachycarpus oreophilus, *in habitat, Doi Chiang Dao, N. Thailand.*
Right: The infructescence with almost ripe fruit.

Trachycarpus princeps
Stone gate palm

Features

From a remote area of China, in fact where China, Tibet, and Burma meet, this most exciting member of the genus grows on near-vertical limestone cliffs high above the Salween River in an area of unspoilt natural beauty. It has a tall, slim, bare trunk, and kidney-shaped seeds, but its most characteristic and unique feature is the brilliant white waxy underside to the fan-shaped leaves, which make it instantly recognizable. A few seeds have come out from this virtually inaccessible area and it is fervently hoped that it will take its place in cultivation in the not too distant future.

Cultivation

There seem to be no problems with growing this beautiful palm, apart from the paucity of seeds. These germinate readily, and the young seedlings grow quite fast, soon producing character leaves. The silver backs are noticeable at a very young age. It should be rather hardy to cold, in common with others in the genus.

Above: Toby Spanner with Trachycarpus princeps, *in habitat, Yunnan, China.*
Right: The leaf underside has a thick coating of white wax.

Trachycarpus takil

Kumaon mountain palm

Features

Once rather common in habitat, this palm is
now all but wiped out by the locals who cut
down the fibrous trunks to make ropes. They
grow, or at least grew, on Mount Thalkedar,
near Pithoraghar in northern India and were
described by Beccari. They are superficially
similar to *T. fortunei* but generally bigger in all
their parts, and have a twisted hastula where
the leaf stalk meets the blade. The seeds are kidney-shaped, blue-black when ripe,
the flowers yellow, and the trunk usually fibrous. Recently a new population is
reported to have been found on the other side of the border from Pithoragarh, in
extreme western Nepal.

Cultivation

All seeds grown thus far are from cultivated trees, and no
seeds from the wild have yet been introduced. With the
discovery of the new population, hopefully this will
change. The seeds germinate easily and seedling growth
is fast and reliable.

Above: Trachycarpus takil, *semi-cultivated, Mt.Thalkedar, Uttar Pradesh,*
India.
Left: The ripe fruits are kidney-shaped.

Trachycarpus wagnerianus

Miniature chusan palm

Features

Not known from the wild, all plants in cultivation are themselves from cultivated trees. They were originally introduced into Europe from Japan early last century, but have remained in comparative obscurity until recently, when their qualities as garden plants were at last realized.

The striking characteristic about "waggies" is their small and stiff leaves, much tougher and more wind tolerant than *T. fortunei,* which it may well replace in popularity as soon as it becomes more widely available. The small leaves give it a jaunty and attractive look. The trunk is fibrous and the fruits are kidney-shaped and blue-black when ripe.

Cultivation

The seeds germinate within a few weeks and the first few leaves may be distorted. After this stage, the young plants grow rapidly and show their true characteristics. Very hardy to cold they are the perfect palm for the smaller, or windier temperate garden.

Above: Trachycarpus wagnerianus, *cultivated, garden of Pauleen Sullivan, Ventura, CA, USA.*
Left: The leaves of young plants rimmed with frost.

Trithrinax acanthocoma

Brazilian needle palm

Features

A small genus of just a few species, though opinions vary as to exactly how many. They are South American palms of the open savanna and dry woodland. This species, widespread in southern Brazil, has a stout, solitary trunk to about 40 feet (12m) tall, which is covered with an interesting and intricate pattern formed by old leaf bases and spines that, near the crown, are upright. The leaves themselves are large and fan-shaped, stiff, green on both surfaces, and from a distance the general appearance is not unlike *Trachycarpus fortunei*, until the spines are seen on the trunk. The fruits are round, ¾ inch (2cm) in diameter, and white when ripe.

Cultivation

Very easy to grow, the seeds germinate fast and the seedlings grow reasonably quickly. The spines on the trunk soon become apparent, even in young plants. Rather hardy, it is well worth trying in temperate gardens, where it will tolerate some frost.

Above: Trithrinax acanthocoma, *cultivated, Les Cedres, Cap Ferat, France.*
Right: The yellow fruits hang down like grapes.

Trithrinax campestris
Caranday palm

Features
Dramatic, clustering palm from Argentina, the trunks of which are covered in spines in an attractive pattern like countless downward pointing pairs of scissors. It grows across a very wide area, but is being relentlessly cleared for farmland, for the growing of sunflowers and soya. Thousands are destroyed every month. It grows to some 23 feet (7m) tall, and a clump may contain five or six trunks. The small, blue-green fan leaves are incredibly stiff, almost metal-like, and sharply pointed at the tips. The yellow flowers are fragrant and appear among the leaves, the fruits which follow are round, about ¾ inch (2cm) in diameter and yellow when ripe.

Cultivation
Many palms are "rescued" from clearances and exported to Europe where they grace the gardens of the well-heeled. From seed, they are very slow growing, taking many years to form a trunk. Extremely hardy to cold.

Above: Trithrinax campestris, *in habitat, San Luis, Argentina.*
Right: The spines look like downward pointing pairs of scissors.
Left: The yellow flowers attract bees.

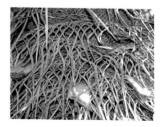

Trithrinax
schizophylla
Mosquito palm

Features

Brazil, Paraguay, Argentina, and Bolivia are the countries where this amazing palm grows, in dry savanna or in light, open thorn forest. They can be either solitary or clustered, and grow to about 15 feet (5m) tall. The trunks are covered with old leaf bases

and spines, some of which can be over 3 feet (1m) long, presenting an extraordinary sight. The leaves are very stiff and fan-shaped, blue-green, and spine tipped. The inflorescences arise among the leaves and the fragrant flowers are yellow. These are followed by round fruits about ½ inch (1cm) or more in diameter, pale yellow when ripe.

Cultivation

Though the fierce armament would be seen by some as a detriment to use, well positioned and out of harm's way, this

would be a valuable addition to any collection. Extremely hardy to cold and wind, it may be tried in the sheltered temperate garden. From seed, it is very slow.

Top: Trithrinax schizophylla, *in habitat, Chuquisaca, Bolivia.*
Above left: The spines can be 3 feet (1m) long.
Left: Unripe fruits.

Verschaffeltia splendida

Features

"Splendid" is indeed an ideal word to describe this fabulous palm, one of a number that occur only on the Seychelle Islands in the Indian Ocean, where it grows inland on hillsides in tropical forest. It grows to about 30 feet (10m) tall and the trunk is slim and spiny with stilt roots, which support it at the base. The leaves attract most attention however as they are entire, unless damaged by the wind, about 6½ feet (2m) long and 3 feet (1m) wide. In exposed locations they appear feather-shaped as they split along the folds. The inflorescences appear below the leaves and carry round fruits ⅔ inch (1½cm) in diameter, brown-green when ripe. These contain the seed, which is hard and ridged and furrowed in a unique way.

Cultivation

If sown fresh the seeds germinate easily in a few weeks, and the seedlings which follow grow steadily. Definitely one for the tropical garden, out of the wind.

Above: Verschaffeltia splendida, *cultivated, Singapore Botanic Garden.*
Left: Older plants develop stilt roots.

Wallichia densiflora

Features

A small, clustering feather-leaved palm from the lower Himalayan mountains in northern India, Nepal, and Bhutan, where it grows on slopes in wet forest at rather high altitudes. Several stems form a clump which grows to about 10 feet (3m) in height. The leaves are arching, the leaflets reminiscent of those of the fishtail palms, diamond-shaped with rough edges, glossy green above and brilliant silvery white beneath. The flowerstalks arise among, and are hidden by, the leaves and after flowering, produce small round fruits about ½ inch (1cm) in diameter and brown when ripe.

Cultivation

The small round seeds germinate erratically over a period of months and need to be sown fresh for the best chance of success. It is a small, pretty palm ideal for the sheltered and shady garden in warm-temperate to subtropical climates, in rich and moist soil. It will even take light frosts.

Above: Wallichia densiflora, cultivated, garden of Orchid Retreat, Kalimpong, W. Bengal, India.
Left: The young inflorescences.

Wallichia disticha
Wallich's palm

Features

Unique and imposing palm from north India where it grows in hilly districts in the foothills of the Himalayas. It grows to 20 feet (6m) in height and the plumose, feather leaves are arranged in two opposite ranks, giving the plant a two-dimensional look, making it easily recognizable. The fibrous trunk is covered with an interesting pattern of old leaf bases, forming close against it. Wallich's palm is very fast growing and soon reaches maturity. The flowerstalks appear among the leaf bases and after flowering produce round fruits, ⅔ inch (1.5cm) in diameter and dark red when ripe.

Cultivation

The small half round seeds germinate easily and quickly. This is a wonderful palm for the botanic garden, however it dies after flowering and fruiting. Its great speed of growth means it would need to be replaced every few years. It grows in climates from temperate to sub-tropical.

Above: Wallichia disticha, *semi-cultivated, Kalimpong-Darjeeling road, W. Bengal, India.*

Right: The huge infructescence contains thousands of seeds.

Far right: The woody trunk patterns.

Washingtonia filifera
Californian cotton palm

Features
Very commonly planted in warm climates all over the world as a street tree, it is one of the most familiar palms. It has a thick trunk up to about 3 feet (1m) in diameter and a height of up to 70 feet (20m). Occurring in southwestern USA and Mexico, it prefers deserts though requires permanent access to ground water, which it will tap with its very long roots. The leaves are big and fan-shaped, green on both surfaces, and with green thorns on the petioles. Old dead leaves hang down, sometimes forming a skirt, which may cover the entire length of the trunk. After flowering, the long, arching, thin flowerstalks produce huge quantities of small round fruits, black when ripe.

Cultivation
Growing this palm could hardly be easier. The seeds germinate within days of sowing and the young plants grow quickly. It is the nurseryman's dream, accounting for its huge popularity or even over use.

Left: Washingtonia filifera *in habitat, Palm Canyon, Borrego Desert State Park, CA, USA.*

Washingtonia robusta

Skyduster palm

Features

Slimmer than *Washingtonia filifera*, the trunk is only half the thickness, though it too may be covered with a thick layer of dead leaves. It grows taller too and may reach over 130 feet (40m) in height. The big fan shaped leaves are green on both surfaces, though there is a noticeable pale brown patch around the point where the leaf stalk joins the blade on the underside. The thorns on the petiole are brown. The inflorescences grow from among the leaves and extend beyond them. The round fruits are black when ripe. This species is from north-western Mexico and is more commonly planted than *W. filifera*.

Cultivation

The small seeds sprout like grass and plants are produced by the thousand for chainstore sale. Best in climates from warm-temperate to tropical. In cooler areas, this species seems more tolerant of damp or wet conditions, though *W. filifera* may be the more cold-tolerate.

Above: Washingtonia robusta, *cultivated, Orto
    Botanico, Naples, Italy.*
*Right: The beige patch can be clearly seen on the
    young leaves.*

Wodyetia bifurcata
Foxtail palm

Features

Discovered and described comparatively recently, this beautiful palm is from Queensland in Australia, where it grows in hot districts, among boulders. It grows up to 40 feet (12m), the solitary trunk is slim and covered with ringlike scars where old leaves have dropped, and there is a crown-shaft. The leaves are dense and plumose, like a huge bottle brush or fox tail. The inflorescences grow from below the crownshaft and produce large quantities of oval fruits to about 2 inches (5cm) long, red when ripe, so heavy they are often supported on cultivated trees in case the weight should break them off.

Cultivation

The seeds are covered with unique bifurcat-ing filaments and germinate easily enough in from two to three months. Seedlings grow rather fast and these palms are now begin-ning to be seen in great numbers in all sub-tropical countries. It makes a superb land-scape subject.

Above: Wodyetia bifurcata, cultivated, National Tropical
*   Botanical Garden, Kalaheo, Kauai, Hawaii.*
Right: The big fruits are red when ripe.

Palms

Zombia antillarum

Zombie palm

Features

Unusual palm whose unique trunk is often passed by, unnoticed among the leaves. From the Dominican Republic and Haiti, where it grows on hillsides, it is a suckering species, the height of which is up to only about 10 feet (3m) tall. The stems are slim and covered with an intricate pattern of spines and fibers, which make it unmistakable. The round fan-shaped leaves are white on the underside and green above. The flowerstalks are produced among the leaves and grow round fruits about ¾ inch (2cm) in diameter and are white when ripe. Altogether a charming small palm ideal for the garden in subtropical to tropical climates.

Cultivation

The seeds are small and round and should be planted fresh. They will germinate in two or three months and seedlings grow rather slowly. They require bright but indirect light and should be potted on as required.

Above: Zombia antillarum, cultivated, Montgomery Botanical Center, Florida, USA.
Left: Often hidden by the leaves, the trunk has an intricate pattern.

A Pocket Guide to Palms

Cycads

Introduction

Superficially, cycads resemble palms, and many plant enthusiasts are attracted equally to both. Botanically, however, they are quite distinct not only from palms, but from every other plant group and represent a plant order unrelated to any other. They are much older and more primitive than palms and appeared on the planet some 200 million years ago. Related more to conifers than any other plants, they produce cones, and male and female are on separate plants. Pollination is carried out either by wind or by insects (or, increasingly, artificially) and, if successful, results in the production of large seeds.

Most cycads are endangered in the wild, some critically so. Agricultural practices are largely responsible for this, but predation by collectors has also played a part; rare species can exchange hands for thousands of dollars. For this reason all cycads are now protected by C.I.T.E.S. (Convention on International Trade in Endangered Species) and licenses are required to both export and import them. Additionally, countries where they grow often have their own internal laws aimed at protecting them. Fortunately, because of the realization of their critical state, extreme measures are now being taken to maintain wild populations, including electronic tagging and heavy fining or even imprisonment of those caught removing them from the wild or illegally exporting them. Even the seeds of many are protected, and with good reason, however, it must be added that many are now produced in cultivation, and legally supply a growing market.

There are thought to be some 200 species of cycad, a mere shadow of the huge populations that once formed a dominant feature of the planet's early flora. We are lucky to have even these and it is hoped that increasing awareness of their beauty and form, as well as their plight, will result in a steady increase in the numbers and profile of these ancient and primitive plants, to the benefit of us all.

This section covers but twenty four species and is intended only as a brief

glimpse at this exciting plant group. Those whose appetite is whetted would do well to sample other books on the subject, some of which are listed in the bibliography. Visitors to South Africa should not miss the Botanic Garden in Durban, which boasts an excellent collection of these "living fossils."

Page 227: Cycads are survivors from a bygone age.

Above: Like conifers, cycads produce cones for seed and pollen production.

Bowenia serrulata

Features

From a genus of two or three species, this unusual small cycad grows in one tiny area in southeastern Queensland, Australia, where it occurs in open forest in wet or dry situations. It is known as the Byfield fern as the population is centered in that area, and because of the frond-like development of the leaves. These are doubly pinnate, the small leaflets roughly diamond shaped with pointed tips, and glossy green with toothed margins, a key identification characteristic. The large underground rootstock has many crowns and may be divided to propagate the plant. It grows to only about 3 or 6½ feet (1 or 2m) in height and the spreading leaves can be up to 6½ feet (2m) long and 3 feet (1m) wide. The seeds are ¾ or 1 inch (2 or 3cm) long, oval in shape, and creamy white when ripe.

Cultivation

Store fresh seed for two to three months, then soak for 24 hours. Half bury in damp sand until germination is noticed. Pot on as required.

Right: Bowenia serrulata,
cultivated, Durban Botanic
Garden, South Africa.

A Pocket Guide to Palms

Bowenia spectabilis

Features

Closely related to *Bowenia serrulata*, this small cycad occurs further north, on the east coast on Cape York Peninsular in Australia. It too has an underground stem, in this case shaped like a carrot with a small number of crowns growing from it. The bipinnate leaves can be up to 6½ feet (2 m) long by 3 feet (1m) wide, the diamond shaped leaflets are glossy green, and the leaf edges are smooth as opposed to toothed.

Cultivation

Fresh seeds should be stored for two to three months to enable them to ripen fully and soaked for 24 hours prior to planting. They should be half-buried on their sides on the substrate (damp sand is best) in a warm but not hot temperature until the emergence of the first root. When this is noticed, the individual seed can be removed and potted up, and placed in a brighter location, though out of sunlight. The rootstock may also be divided.

Right: Bowenia spectabilis,
*cultivated, Durban Botanic
Garden, South Africa.*

Ceratozamia mexicana

Features

Genus of about fifteen species of Central American cycads. This species grows in eastern Mexico in forests at low elevations or on sometimes steep mountainsides, where it is locally common and clearly visible from the road. The pinnate leaves are up to 3 feet (1m) long and dark green, the leaflets are narrow and pointed at the tip. Older plants may form a short trunk or this may be subterranean. Plants grow to about 5 to 6½ feet (1.5 to 2m) tall and the leaves are held upright. The cones are cylinder-shaped; male and female are on separate plants, and the seeds are pinkish-whitish when ripe.

Cultivation

All flesh should be removed and the seeds stored for a few weeks to allow after-ripening. Half plant the seeds on their sides in moist sand and germination should take place rather quickly. Remove the seed as soon as this occurs and plant them up into individual pots in a brighter spot, avoiding direct sunlight.

Left: The new leaves of Ceratozamia *are pinky-bronze on some species.*

Cycas panzhihuaensis

Dukou cycad

Features

The genus *Cycas* contains about fifty species, distributed from Africa to Southeast Asia, China, and Australia. *Dukou cycad* comes from a small area in central China and is named for Panzhihua City, a desperately polluted coal mining and steel smelting area, a tribute to this plant's resilience. It is used there in parks and gardens and is said by some to be the most numerous cycad in the world, though it is rare outside China. It grows to about 6½ feet (2m) tall, and the trunk is some 12 inches (30cm) in diameter. The leaves are dark bluish-green and held flat. The oval seeds are an inch (2.5cm) long and red when ripe.

Cultivation

Fresh seeds should be allowed to mature from six to twelve months after collection, then soaked, cleaned of all flesh and half planted on their sides, on damp sand. They may take some months to germinate, or it may happen quickly. Extremely cold-tolerant, it can withstand severe frosts.

Above: Cycas panzhihuaensis, *cultivated, Panzhihua City, China.*

Right: The trunk is covered with old leaf bases.

Cycas pectinata

Features

This cycad originates from northern India and Thailand, and much of Southeast Asia, where it grows at elevations of up to 3,000 feet (1,000m) in light, open forests, sometimes pine, with tropical wet climates. It grows a lumpy trunk up to 40 feet (12m) in height, sometimes branched, covered with the scars of old leaf bases. Some of the taller trunks must be extremely old. The leaves are mid-green, 5 feet (1.5m) long by about 12 inches (30cm) wide, and the leaflets are narrow and closely spaced. The seeds are large, about 2 inches (5cm) long, oval in shape, and bright orange when ripe.

Cultivation

Fully ripe seeds must be soaked and all signs of flesh should be removed prior to sowing. The seed should be laid on its side and pressed into damp sand that is kept moist. They will sprout in a few weeks, given a little heat. Pot up individually as required and move to a brighter location. It is not cold-tolerant, but makes an attractive indoor plant.

Left: Cycas pectinata, *in habitat, Doi Chiang Dao, N. Thailand.*

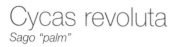

Cycas revoluta
Sago "palm"

Features

The most common and best known cycad, it is widely available in nurseries and chainstores around the world. Occurring naturally on a few islands off the coast of Japan, it has been cultivated for 150 years. It can grow to 10 feet (3m) or more tall with a branching trunk approximately 12 inches (30cm) in diameter. The leaves are flatly held, 3 feet (1m) long and 8 inches (20cm) wide, and the leaflets are glossy dark green and closely spaced. The female cone is large and spherical, the male long and elongated. The seeds are red when ripe and about 1 inch (3cm) long, and oval in shape.

Cultivation

When the seeds are fully ripe they should be soaked in warm water for a day or so. This will enable the seed to absorb water, but will also make the removal of the flesh much easier. Germination should occur within a few weeks. This species is quite hardy and large specimens can take several degrees of frost.

Above: Cycas revoluta, *cultivated, Barcelona, Spain.*
Left: The new leaves grow very quickly.

Dioon edule

Features

One of a genus of ten species from rocky areas in Mexico and Honduras, *D. edule* is well-known in cultivation and is an attractive plant. The solitary trunk grows ultimately to some 10 feet (3m) tall by about 12 inches (30cm) diameter, usually unbranched. The leaves are blue-green and the stiff, narrow, pointed leaflets are so closely spaced as to be sometimes overlapping, presenting a distinctive and pleasing appearance. The male cone is cylindrical, the female oval in shape, and the seeds white when ripe.

Cultivation

Seed can be germinated either by laying them flat on moist sand or by the "bag method" usually used for palms. Mix the seeds with moist peat and place in a clear plastic bag, which is then sealed and labeled. Germination takes place in a few weeks if seeds are fully ripe, and can be seen through the plastic. Remove sprouted seeds and pot up. This species is rather cold-hardy and tolerates several degrees of frost when larger.

Above: Dioon edule, *cultivated, Fairchild Tropical Garden, Miami, Florida, USA.*

Dioon
spinulosum

Features

From the south of Mexico, where it grows in evergreen woodland of conifers, in limestone ravines. It grows a stout trunk about 16 inches (40cm) in diameter and 30 feet (10m) or more tall. Specimens with 50 feet (15m) of trunk have been reported. The leaves comprise a rounded crown and are glossy green, about 3 or 6½ feet (1 or 2m) long, and arching. The leaflets, as the name suggests, are bordered with sharp spines, five or six along each side. The male cone is erect and tapering, the female broadly conical, pendulous, and hanging down from among the leaves. The seeds are oval, about 1½ inches (4cm) long, and white when ripe.

Cultivation

The large seeds should be cleaned of flesh and allowed to fully ripen before sowing. Soak for 24 hours, then lay them flat on damp sand, and press in lightly, a deep pot is best. They germinate within a few weeks and the seedlings grow quickly.

Above: Dioon spinulosum, *cultivated, Montgomery Botanical Center, Florida.*
Left: The female cone.

Encephalartos bubalinus

Features

One of a large genus of over fifty species restricted to Africa, *E. bubalinus* is a smallish species from Tanzania, which grows to only about 6½ feet (2m) tall on quartz and granite hills at some altitude. The trunk is about 16 inches (40cm) in diameter and produces basal suckers which may be removed for propagation. The glossy, mid-green leaves are 3 feet (1m) long by 8 or 12 inches (20 or 30cm) wide and are arranged in a hemispherical crown. The male cones are tall and tapering, like a slim pine cone, the females are barrel-shaped, green, and sit horizontally in the crown of leaves. The seeds are yellow or orange when ripe.

Cultivation

Encephalartos seeds take quite a long time to ripen and even after falling may need a further six months or more before they are ready to sow. This should be done using the traditional method, that is half burying the cleaned and soaked seeds in moist sand. After they are seen to sprout, they should be potted up using an open soil mix.

Above: Encephalartos bubalinus, *cultivated, Montgomery Botanical Center, Florida.*
Right: The female cone.

A Pocket Guide to Palms

Encephalartos eugene-maraisii

Features

This is a beautiful, stiff-leaved species, the leaflets are blue-green and grow at a sharp angle to the leaf stem, giving each leaf a noticeable V-shape. The trunk is stout and covered with old leaf bases and it grows to a few feet in height. From Transvaal in South Africa, the once large populations have been much reduced by uncontrolled collection of mature specimens from the wild. This situation has now been tackled with the electronic tagging of all large plants in habitat, and hopefully the decline in native stocks will decrease. Four or five cones are produced on each stem, the male are cylindrical, the female more rounded; the seeds are pale brown.

Cultivation

They are slow to grow from seed, which encourages wild collection. The seeds should be stored for a few months to allow them to fully ripen, then pressed into moist sand. With luck, they should sprout in a few weeks, or months. Subsequent seedling growth is slow.

Left: Encephalartos eugene-maraisii, *cultivated, Durban Botanic Garden, South Africa.*

Encephalartos ferox

Features

One of the more widely available and easily grown African cycads, it occurs naturally in the northeast of South Africa and in adjoining Mozambique, where it grows in open evergreen forest close to the coast and even on sandy beaches among other plants. The trunk may be underground, or emergent to 3 feet (1m) or more tall. The dark green leaves are erect or held flat, and are broad with wavy and spiny edges, reminiscent of holly. The cones are bright orange-red, the male erect and cylindrical, the female barrel-shaped with a rounded point at the top, and there may be several per stem in each case. The seeds are red when ripe.

Cultivation

Ripen the seeds, clean and soak them, before sowing. They should germinate in a few weeks or months. The seedlings grow relatively fast, and make good house- or conservatory plants, or can be grown outdoors in the tropical or subtropical garden.

Above: Encephalartos ferox, *cultivated, Durban Botanic Garden, South Africa.*
Left: The female cone.

Encephalartos gratus

Features

From Malawi and Mozambique, this large and rare cycad suckers profusely around the base of the, up to 10 feet (3m) tall, 24 inches (60cm) thick, trunk. On cultivated plants these may be removed for propagation. The leaves are held flat or erect and the leaflets, a glossy green, are rather twisted, spine edged and irregular, giving the whole plant a somewhat untidy look. The cones are bright orange-red and may number from five to twenty per stem. The male cones are cylindrical, the female ones too, though they are thicker and more barrel-shaped.

Cultivation

Fresh seeds need several months to continue ripening and maturing. After this they should be soaked and cleaned. Sowing is accomplished by pressing them sideways on, into damp sand. Using this method, germination may be anticipated within a few weeks or months. Remove the sprouts and pot up individually. *E. gratus* is suitable for a tropical or subtropical climate and, like other *Encephalartos*, makes a good potted specimen when young.

Above: Encephalartos gratus, cultivated, Montgomery Botanical Center, Florida, USA.
Left: The female cone.

Encephalartos horridus

Features

This extraordinary species has blue, twisted, and spiny leaves forming an impenetrable thicket in parts of the Eastern Cape, where it occurs on ridges and hills of quartzite. It is a once seen never forgotten cycad, which grows to less than 3 feet (1m) or so, and the leaves form a round crown. The powder blue leaflets are lobed with spines and each is further rolled into a spine tipped tube. It is unfriendly but attractive nonetheless, and much sought after as a pot plant. The cones are one per stem; the male erect and spindle shaped, the female ones are barrel-shaped. The seeds are bright red when ripe.

Cultivation

The seeds germinate easily and rather quickly if treated in the manner described previously. The young plants grow at a reasonable speed and soon show the adult characteristics. They make showy indoor plants for the hot, dry conservatory.

Right: Encephalartos horridus, *Durban Botanic Garden, South Africa.*

Encephalartos lehmannii

Features

The blue form is perhaps the bluest of all the cycads, its smooth, spineless leaflets give it an attractive look and it is popular as a houseplant. There is also a green leaved form, less showy but nice-looking nonetheless. It grows a trunk to about 6½ feet (2m) high by about 12 or 16 inches (30 or 40cm) in diameter. The leaves are approximately 5 feet (1.5m) long, carried erect, and the stiff leaflets are held upright, altogether producing the effect of a tough and sturdy plant, which undoubtedly it is. Male and female cones are produced one per stem, spindle, and barrel-shaped respectively. Seeds are oblong, up to 2 inches (5cm) long, and bright red when ripe.

Cultivation

Illegal collection in the wild has undoubtedly supplied many cultivated plants. From seed, patience is required as, even at the best of times, they are slow to form any trunk. However, the seeds do germinate quickly and far-sighted growers are producing more and more for sale.

Above: Encephalartos lehmannii, *cultivated, Durban Botanic Garden, South Africa.*

Encephalartos manikensis

Features

From Zimbabwe and Mozambique, where it grows on spectacular granite hillsides and is locally very common, this attractive cycad grows a short thick trunk to only about 6½ feet (2m) in height. The thorny, glossy, dark green leaves grow in a rounded crown. Male and female cones are on separate plants, and similar in shape, though the female is much shorter and thicker than the male. They are rather variable in size and occur in shades of green. The seeds, about 1 inch (3cm) long, are oval and red when ripe.

Cultivation

The oval seeds take up to six months to fully ripen and should be stored before planting. Soaking will re-hydrate the embryo and will make removing the flesh much easier. The seeds should be pressed into moist sand and should germinate in a few weeks or months, at which point they should be potted up. Because of their habitat, adult plants can take full sun and much heat.

Above: Encephalartos manikensis, *cultivated, Fairchild Tropical Garden, Florida.*
Left: The female cone.

A Pocket Guide to Palms

Lepidozamia hopei

Features

From a genus of but two species, originating in eastern Australia, *L. hopei* occurs in rainforests in wet ground, a clue to its requirements in cultivation. From northeast Queensland, it is a handsome plant with a 20 inch (50cm) diameter trunk that grows up to 70 feet (20m) in height, making it among the tallest growing cycads in the world. The dark green, glossy leaves can be 6½ or 10 feet (2 or 3m) long by up to 20 inches (50cm) wide, finely pinnate, without spines, and the leaflets closely spaced. The dissimilar cones are one per stem; the male cylindrical, the female oval in shape. The seeds are oblong, about 2 inches (5cm) long by ¾ inch (2cm) wide, and they are bright red.

Cultivation

This rarely seen cycad is the less common of the two in the genus. Sow the seeds after ripening and cleaning. They should sprout within a few weeks and may be potted up immediately.

Above: Lepidozamia hopei, *cultivated, Daintree area, Queensland, Australia.*
Right: Fruiting female cone.

Lepidozamia peroffskyana

Features

This species occurs in south-east Queensland, further south than *Lepidozamia hopei*. It grows in rich soils and wet situations in rainforests. It too is a tall-growing species, though not more than to 20 feet (6m). The thick trunk is about 16 inches (40cm) in diameter and covered with thousands of diamond-shaped scars of fallen leaves, indicating the great age of some of these dinosaur-like plants. The leaves are about 6½ feet (2m) long, shiny and mid- to dark green. The leaflets are narrow and pointed at the tip and closely and regularly spaced along the rachis. The cones are as for *L. hopei*. The seeds are 2 inches (5cm) long, by about ¾ to 1 inch (2 to 3cm) wide, and bright red.

Cultivation

Its habitat indicates its requirements once established: plenty of water and a rich soil. Pot grown plants are pretty and fairly fast growing and make good house- or conservatory plants while young.

Above: Lepidozamia peroffskyana, *in habitat, Queensland, Australia.*
Right: The male cone.

Macrozamia communis

Features

A large genus of some twenty species all of which are from Australia, where they occur in light open forest or on dry ridges and mountain slopes. This species is from southeast Australia, in New South Wales, where it forms dense colonies on

mountainsides and ridges, or sometimes in sandy situations near the coast. Usually the trunk is absent or below ground, but very old plants can grow a solitary trunk up to 6½ feet (2m) in height. The leaves are plentiful and finely pinnate, and form a rounded, elegant soft-looking crown. The male cones are cylindrical; the female ones barrel-shaped, both blue-green, and there may be more than one cone per stem. Seeds are no more than 1 inch (3cm) long, oval, and bright red when ripe.

Cultivation

Store very fresh seeds for a month before sowing to allow them to fully mature. Great plants for garden or home/conservatory, but slow growing.

Left: Macrozamia communis, *in habitat, New South Wales, Australia.*

Macrozamia moorei

Features

A stunning species with a single, massive trunk up to 3 feet (1m) in diameter and 20 feet (7m) in height, which is covered with countless thousands of diamond-shaped scars, each one representing a fallen leaf. It occurs in colonies, sometimes dense, in central Queensland in dry open forest and on rocky ridges. The leaves are numerous, finely pinnate, hard and glossy, forming an elegant, rounded crown.

The male cones are cylindrical and numerous, the female cones wider and thicker, just a few per stem. The seeds are oval, up to 2 inches (5cm) long, and bright red when ripe.

Cultivation

Cultivate as other cycads, allowing a month or so for the fresh seeds to fully ripen. After the flesh has been soaked off they can be sown either in a bag of moist peat, or on their sides pressed into damp sand. Germination is fast, but the seedlings grow slowly. Full-size wild plants are being exported with full C.I.T.E.S. authority to Europe, where they fetch a high price.

Left: Macrozamia moorei, *cultivated, Fairchild Tropical Garden, Florida, USA.*

Microcycas calocoma

Features

This species, from a tiny area in western Cuba, where it is thankfully heavily protected, is in a genus of its own. A most attractive plant, extremely rare in cultivation, it grows a trunk up to 30 feet (10m) in height and 1½ feet (0.5m) in diameter. Its unique characteristic is the drooping nature of the leaflets, which hang down either side of the rachis and at a slight angle to it. The tip of the leaf has an open-ended, cut-off look. The yelow cones are cylindrical, the female broader than the male. The seeds are 1 or 1½ inches (3 or 4cm) long, and red when ripe.

Cultivation

Any opportunity to grow this exciting cycad should not be missed, though some patience is required. Fresh seeds should be stored for a month to allow them to fully ripen, and young plants should be potted up into an open mix. Plants of any size are extremely valuable.

Above: Microcycas calocoma, *cultivated, Montgomery Botanical Center, Florida, USA.*

Right: The female cone.

Stangeria eriopus

Features

Stangeria is a genus of one very interesting species. It occurs naturally in southeastern South Africa on often sandy soils near the coast. It was originally considered to be a fern. When one produced a cone in an English botanic garden, the mistake was realized. It is an attractive plant with soft looking pale green pinnate leaves and an underground stem from which a number of crowns may grow. This may be carefully divided to propagate the plant. The male cone is narrow and cylindrical, the female egg-shaped. The seeds are dark red when ripe.

Cultivation

Fully mature seeds should be soaked for 24 hours and all flesh removed. The damp sand method works well for *Stangeria* and the seed should be pressed half way into the sand. Germination should occur within a few weeks or months. As soon as it is observed, the young plant should be removed and potted up into a light, open soil mix.

Right: Stangeria eriopus, *cultivated, Durban Botanic Garden, South Africa.*

Zamia furfuracea

Cardboard zamia

Features

One of a large and widespread genus of fifty or sixty species from the north of South America, through Central America, and into Mexico, Florida, and some Caribbean Islands. Named for its tough and leathery leaves, the Cardboard zamia is widely available as a pot or houseplant, and as such performs well. From Veracruz in Mexico, it has a branching underground stem which produces several crowns of leaves. These have roughly diamond-shaped leaflets, thick and leathery. In sunny situations these are really crowded and overlap each other. The male cone is cylindrical, the female is barrel-shaped and produces small, bright red seeds.

Cultivation

The seeds are among the easiest of any cycad to germinate and grow, so this makes a good beginner's choice. They sprout easily, using either the bag method or on damp sand, and the young plants grow satisfyingly quickly.

Above: Cardboard zamia is named for its leaves.

Left: Zamia furfuracea, *cultivated, The Palm Centre, Richmond, UK.*

Zamia pseudoparasitica

Features

An extraordinary and unique cycad which grows as an epiphyte on forest trees in coastal Panama. The seeds are thought to be distributed by birds or bats and take firm root in the trunk, with many small fibrous roots spreading to take the increasing weight. It grows a small trunk and the 3 to 10 feet (1 to 3m) long leaves, with glossy, mid-green, pointed leaflets, hang down from the tree. The cones are similar,

with the male being narrower than the female and these are upright within the crown. The seeds are oval, ¾ inch (2cm) long, and yellow when ripe.

Cultivation

Not much is known about the requirements of these rare cycads, but as they only grow in trees, a hanging basket would probably suit them best, in light shade in the tropical garden. Rarely seen in cultivation outside a few botanic gardens, any special effort to grow this unusual plant would be richly rewarded.

Left: Zamia pseudoparasitica, *cultivated, Montgomery Botanical Center, Florida, USA.*

Zamia skinneri

Features

From gloomy Central American rainforests, this wonderful and rare understory plant slowly grows a slim trunk, either underground or up to 6½ feet (2m) tall, from which emerge a few 3 or 6½ feet (1 or 2m) long leaves with widely spaced, large, roughly diamond-shaped leaflets, which can be up to an amazing 20 inches (50cm), but are more usually seen about 8 inches (20cm). long. These are corrugated or grooved along their length, glossy and mid-green. The petioles are lined with sparse thorns. The cones are several per plant and the female is much larger than the male. The red seeds are about ¾ inch (2 cm) long, and oval.

Cultivation

Seeds are not often available of this unusual cycad, so any opportunity to obtain them should be taken. The seeds take some months to germinate and the seedlings grow slowly, though soon displaying the characteristic glossy leaf.

Right: Zamia skinneri,
cultivated, Montgomery
Botanical Center,
Florida, USA.

Bibliography and Glossary

As may be imagined, many authors are referred to in the writing of a book. Some of the most important are listed here:

Boyer, Keith, 1992: *Palms and Cycads Beyond the Tropics*

Dransfield, John & Natalie Uhl, 1987: *Genera Palmarum*

Goode, Douglas, 2001: *Cycads of Africa*

Henderson, Andrew, and others, 1995: *Field Guide to the Palms of the Americas*

Jones, David, 1993: *Cycads of the World*

Jones, David, 1995: *Palms Throughout the World*

Tuley, Paul, 1995: *The Palms of Africa*

The International Palm Society, Lawrence, Kansas, publish a quarterly journal, *PALMS*, to whom all palm enthusiasts are highly recommended.

Visit their website at *www.palms.org*

In Europe, the European Palm Society's magazine, *Chamaerops*, is also published quarterly.

Write for details to *EPS, c/o The Palm Centre, Ham Central Nursery, Ham Street, Ham, Richmond, Surrey, TW10 7HA, UK*. Website *www.palmsociety.org*

After-ripening	The period required for cycad seeds to fully ripen, after they have fallen from the parent plant.
Bi-pinnate	Of the leaf, twice divided, doubly pinnate.
Bract	A modified leaf which covers the flower stalk.
Costapalmate	Having the leaf stalk running into the blade.
Crownshaft	The leaf bases of some palms are formed into a tube that clasps the trunk.
Entire	Of the leaf, unsplit, undivided.
Hastula	A small crest, where the petiole meets the blade.
Inflorescence	The palm's flowering structure.
Infructescence	The stem of the palm which carries the fruit.
Palmate	Of the leaf, hand or fan-shaped.
Petiole	The section of leaf stem between the trunk and the blade.
Pinnate	Of the leaf, feather-shaped.
Rachis	The section of leaf stem beyond the petiole, which carries the blade or leaflets.
Tomentum	Fibrous scales or scurf, usually white, covering leaf or petiole.

Latin Names Index

Common Names Index